The U.S.
Balance of Payments
and Capital Flows

The U.S. Balance of Payments and Capital Flows

John D. Hogan

FREDERICK A. PRAEGER, Publishers
New York · Washington · London

The purpose of the Praeger Special Studies is to make specialized research monographs in U.S. and international economics and politics available to the academic, business, and government communities. For further information, write to the Special Projects Division, Frederick A. Praeger, Publishers, 111 Fourth Avenue, New York, N.Y. 10003.

FREDERICK A. PRAEGER, PUBLISHERS
111 Fourth Avenue, New York, N.Y. 10003, U.S.A.
77-79 Charlotte Street, London W.1, England

Published in the United States of America in 1967
by Frederick A. Praeger, Inc., Publishers

Second printing, 1968

Library of Congress Catalog Card Number: 66-18904

Printed in the United States of America

FOR

TOM AND JIM

PREFACE

This work is an outgrowth of the author's interest in the economic function of capital markets and their importance in international flows of funds. Research studies on European capital market problems, conducted by the author for the Northwestern Mutual Life Insurance Company, intensified this interest and led into studies of the implications for the U.S. balance of payments of apparent deficiencies, in depth and flexibility, of these markets. An exchange of correspondence with several European central banks, following publication of the author's views on European capital market development,[1] resulted in invitations to discuss differences of opinion with the banks' personnel. During the spring of 1965, therefore, the author visited major financial centers in Europe and conducted sessions with officials of the Deutsche Bundesbank, the Deutsche Bank, A.G., the Schweizerische Bankgesellschaft, (Zürich), the Banca d' Italia, the Banque de France, the Rotterdam-Amsterdam Bank, and the Nederlandsche Bank. Such insights as this experience afforded and the stimulation to thought that it provided have, the author hopes, found expression in this analysis of international monetary problems in the postwar period.

The economist, while taking pride in the theoretical conceptual tools built by generations of his colleagues, must sometimes lament that his historian opposites have not developed similar tools. Not all of the events since 1914, or since 1945, have had a bearing upon the plight of world monetary relations; but which events *have* had a bearing, and through what process? Perhaps the historian's skills in narration, coupled with a characteristic expansiveness in exposition (all histories are large volumes), have compensated for lack of theoretical tools. In any case the author has struggled with the frustration that grew out of sensing the importance to present-day world monetary problems of the stream of events that led from the disruption of the international monetary system in the interwar period, through the Second World War, and into the postwar period--yet lacking any guide to which events properly should be selected or rejected--and has relied on his own sensibilities. Neither expansiveness nor narrative skill, the author fears, availed him; the former was eliminated by the standards of size for Praeger Special Studies, and the author dared not rely on the latter. It is hoped that the chapters given over to historical exposition accomplish their minimum objective--to establish the continuity of international monetary problems during the last sixty years.

The author has taken some liberties with tables in Chapter 5. In addition to the usual source information, he has provided a guide to the derivation of the several payments balance concepts now officially used in the United States by keying each payments concept component to its source table(s) in the June, 1966, _Survey of Current Business_. This issue of the _Survey of Current Business_ presents a reorganization of the balance of payments data and incorporates substantial revision of the individual series.

Notes to Preface

1. John D. Hogan, "Western European Capital Markets and the Role of Life Insurance Companies," _Journal of Risk and Insurance_, 31 (June, 1964), pp. 157-68.

_______. "Western European Capital Markets and U.S. Capital Outflow Restriction," _The Quarterly Review of Economics and Business_, 4 (Summer, 1964), pp. 65-78.

ACKNOWLEDGMENTS

The author has been the beneficiary of good friends in the completion of this work. At the urging of Donald C. Slichter, formerly president of the Northwestern Mutual Life Insurance Company, the author determined to draw together for publication several research studies on various aspects of the U.S. balance of payments problem. The late Carl R. Bye, Dean of the Graduate School, Syracuse University, first brought the author's attention to the challenges that lay in international finance. A large number of European acquaintances were helpful "beyond the call" by their hospitality, their willingness to provide data, and their response to queries. The author would be remiss not to acknowledge his obligation to Dr. Franz-Josef Trouvain and Dr. Walter Seipp, of the Deutsche Bank A.G.; Dr. Harald Joerges, of the Deutsche Bundesbank; Dr. Karl W. Hardach, of the Technische Universität Berlin; Dr. Ernst Hausherr, of the Schweizerische Bankgesellschaft, Zürich; Dr. Guiliano Monterastelli, of the Banca d' Italia; Dr. Pierre Berger and Dr. Felíx Aubert, of the Banque de France; Dr. C. F. Karsten, of the Rotterdam-Amsterdam Bank; and Dr. G. A. Kessler, of the Nederlandsche Bank N.V.

The author has been fortunate in the friendship of several persons whose careers have deeply involved them in international economic problems. Valuable assistance and counsel were received by the author from the Honorable Frank M. Coffin, formerly U.S. Representative to the Organisation for Economic Cooperation and Development. The Honorable Henry S. Reuss, Chairman of the Subcommittee on International Exchange and Payments of the Joint Economic Committee, has been a valuable source of ideas and criticism. John Ghiardi and Robert N. Bee, Financial Attachés to the U.S. Embassies in Rome and Bonn, respectively, were generous with their time and good offices.

In the preparation of the manuscript--an altogether unique regimen when, as in the Praeger Special Studies Series, the submitted manuscript is directly reproduced--members of the author's staff at the Northwestern Mutual Life Insurance Company summoned patience hitherto only presumed to reside within them as they composed tables, typed and retyped pages, and finished an arduous task in good spirits. Mrs. Patricia P. Schumacher, aided by Miss Kay A. Schimek, accomplished these wonders. Mrs. Eleanor Foregger proofread the manuscript and made many helpful suggestions.

The patience and helpfulness of Jacquelyn P. Reimann, Managing Editor of the Praeger Special Projects Division, deserve many thanks.

CONTENTS

LIST OF TABLES

Table		Page

The U.S. Balance of Payments and Capital Flows

CHAPTER 1 INTRODUCTION

The year 1958 brought a new realization to the United States of its role in the international monetary system. Deficits in the balance of payments would henceforth constrain its freedom to choose policies, domestic as well as foreign, on the sole criterion of domestic preference. A period of autonomy in policy-making had come to an end.

During the early postwar years, the major trading countries had welcomed U.S. "deficits" (largely government grants and credits) which enabled them to gain access to American producer and consumer goods pending reconstruction of their own economies. With reconstruction completed in the mid-1950's, world merchandise trade and capital movements increased rapidly with the consequence that Western Europe and Japan were able to earn claims on dollars and accumulate dollar reserves. Growing dollar reserves in Western Europe soon attained levels that central banks considered excessive and they began to convert them to gold. From 1958 to 1960 U.S. gold reserves decreased by $2.8 billion and gold reserves of the rest of the world increased by $2.8 billion, of which $2.3 billion was accounted for by West Germany, France and Italy. By 1965 the decrease in the U.S. gold reserves had reached $6.8 billion and the increase in the rest of the world $9.8 billion, of which West Germany, France and Italy accounted for $7.0 billion. An increase of $3.9 billion in total world gold reserves occurred during the 1958-65 period. In addition to the dollar claims converted to gold, official institutions in foreign countries held $14.1 billion of short-term dollar liabilities at the close of 1965, about half by central banks in Western Europe.

The consequences of its deteriorating position in international affairs became increasingly vexing to the United States after 1958. Most important, the choice of economic policy-mix to stimulate the underemployed economy was constrained by the belief that restrictive policies were required to conserve monetary reserves. Despite the occurrence of a recession in 1960 after the briefest expansion in the postwar period and persistence of unemployment at a rate near 6 percent, a program to stimulate the economy was delayed until the second quarter of 1964. Restrictions on policy options affected those policies directed toward external equilibrium as well as those directed toward internal equilibrium. The most confining restrictions arose from the "key currency" role of the dollar. Unlike other currencies, the dollar had become the accounting unit of the international payments system, replacing the pound in this role. International and regional payments systems chose to employ the dollar as a common denominator among member country currencies. Moreover, international accounts were now "balanced" through dollar transfers and the major trading countries were holding part of their monetary reserves in dollar claims. As a consequence, the United States could not change the dollar's value vis-a-vis other currencies without disrupting the entire monetary system.

The United States and the United Kingdom were the architects of the Bretton Woods System, the international monetary system under which the free world nations have operated since 1947. Paradoxically, these two countries, in comparison with other participating countries, have been disadvantaged by the system--in large part because the dollar and the pound have been the chief reserve currencies. This development was not foreseen when the system was established. It was assumed that the adjustment mechanisms within the system would be generally available to member nations to meet the objectives agreed upon at Bretton Woods. The Articles of Agreement of the International Monetary Fund, the institution through which the monetary part of the Bretton Woods system operates, state (Article I) that the objective of the Fund is "to shorten the duration and lessen the degree of disequilibrium in the international balances of payments of members." To accomplish this end the Articles charged the Fund: to promote international monetary cooperation through machinery for consultation and collaboration on international monetary problems; to facilitate the expansion and balanced growth of international trade and contribute thereby to the promotion and maintenance of high levels of employment and real income of all members; to promote exchange stability, maintain orderly exchange arrangements, and avoid competitive exchange depreciation; to assist in the establishment of a multilateral system of payments and the elimination of foreign exchange restrictions; and to give confidence to members by making the Fund's resources available to them under adequate safeguards, thus providing them with the opportunity to correct maladjustments in their balance of payments without resorting to measures destructive of national or international property.

The Bretton Woods system in operation has revealed serious shortcomings that will force its revision or, an improbable alternative, its replacement. The system lacks adequate adjustive mechanisms to correct disequilibrium and fails to provide for the growth of monetary reserves, except if a key currency nation runs persistent deficits in its balance of payments. The survival of the system and the vigorous expansion of international trade during the last ten years have been due less to the IMF machinery than to ad hoc arrangements outside the system, especially the grant and loan policies followed unilaterally by the United States since the end of World War II. Thus far, the decade of the 1960's has seen the emergence of policies that are destructive of international monetary cooperation and, hence, basically alien to the spirit of the Bretton Woods Agreement. Among the major trading countries, differences over relative preferences for full employment, price stability, and government intervention in economic affairs have developed. Unfortunately, the differences are drawn along the lines of surplus or deficit condition in balances of payments. The surplus countries have been unwilling to adopt policies that would reduce their surpluses and relieve deficit countries except to the minimum extent required to keep the dollar-sterling system going.

The resulting line-up among countries, a division that is becoming increasingly rigid, is "surplus countries" versus "deficit countries" and, politically, Continental Europe (Common Market) versus the Sterling Area and the United States. This division of countries despite their essential common interests complicates efforts to reform the system. In November, 1964, the vulnerability of the system was revealed when a sterling crisis developed. Pledges of some $3 billion in credits to support the pound were raised by the Federal Reserve Bank of New York through an all-night "telethon" with leading central banks. This mission is subject to varied interpretations as to whether it demonstrated the strength or weakness of the international payments system. In any case, it is fortunate that, in anticipation of the need, ad hoc procedures for inter-central bank borrowing had been arranged in 1962.

The U.S. deficit on international account since 1958 has been attributable in large part to private capital outflow. Net exports have been large in relation to total exports; and government operations abroad, including economic and military aid, have been increasingly tied to exports. Private capital flows, however, have increased substantially over their previous levels, spurred by the return to convertiblity of the major currencies in 1958 and a low rate of economic growth in the United States relative to Continental Europe and Japan. The policy-mix developed by the United States after 1958 to reduce its deficit has, therefore, been largely concerned with restriction of capital outflow. Such restrictions are permitted under the Bretton Woods Agreement; but their imposition by the United States, the only country whose capital markets had been open to foreign borrowing and whose citizens could freely invest abroad throughout the postwar period, was a reluctant choice.

It was the peculiar misfortune of the United States to be faced with <u>internal</u> disequilibrium at the time of its recognition that it faced external disequilibrium. A flagging rate of growth and persistent unemployment despite general price stability induced increased capital outflow problems at the same time that the external deficit attained record size. In the early 1960's, a policy-mix was developed that included substantial income tax reduction and increased short-term and stabilized long-term interest rates at a moderate level. An economic expansion under way since early 1961 experienced a vigorous renewal after this policy-mix was instituted in early 1964. Judging by the results through 1965, these policies did not have unfortunate effects either on the stability of prices or on the deficit.

With respect to the U.S. external disequilibrium, the mix of policies included some ingenious innovations in foreign exchange operations, changes in taxation of foreign income received by American citizens, promotion of exports, development of non-inflationary wage negotiation guidelines to contain cost-push pressures and, as previously mentioned, restrictions on selective capital exports. The objective was to contain and reduce the deficit and, during the period of improvement, work to revise the Bretton Woods system that made external equilibrium so elusive for a key currency country.

Events thus far in the 1960's have not favored the U.S. strategy. The U.S. balance of payments predicament has been complicated by the emergence of forces unrelated to the international monetary problem that, nonetheless, influence it profoundly. "Le grandeur de la France," the goal of the Fifth Republic under de Gaulle, has led to policies inimical to resolution of the U.S. deficit. The greatest losses of gold reserves during the last five years have occurred as a consequence of French conversion of dollar claims--a total of $2.3 billion. French intransigence on the issue of international monetary reform, moreover, has frustrated positive efforts to revise the Bretton Woods system. To the problem of split ranks among the major trading countries has been added the problem of waging a war on a distant front in Vietnam. The balance of payments impact of the U.S. Vietnam commitment may exceed $1 billion in net payments during 1966, a year that was expected to see the end of the deficit.

This overview of the stresses on the international monetary system sets forth the problem as it is posed to the United States. More extensive treatment of the many issues that have been raised will be given in the chapters that follow. The restriction of capital movements, the chief measure in the policy-mix adopted by the United States to restore equilibrium, and the modifications required in the international monetary system to permit the United States to achieve and maintain equilibrium will be discussed. Substitutes for the Bretton Woods system, pressed vigorously in recent years, will be weighed against the alternative of modifying the prevailing system.

CHAPTER 2 THE ROAD TO BRETTON WOODS

International monetary relations during the years from 1914 to the present exhibit a "paradise lost--paradise regained" character. Lost during the 1914-18 years, and apparently irrecoverable until World War II, was a world monetary system based on the gold standard to which the trading nations had adhered with remarkable fealty. The same trading nations, rent by the destruction of World War I and the animosities that survived it, were unable to restore the old system. During the interwar years, a terrible price was paid for the autarkical policies practiced by the major trading nations: not only decline of world trade, and internal disequilibrium in many countries, but the sowing of the seeds of World War II. Regained in 1944, after the lessons of the interwar period had been learned, was a system--the Bretton Woods System--that restored world monetary relations under more challenging circumstances than those encountered after World War I. Because the Bretton Woods innovations are now being weighed to determine the need for new changes in international monetary institutions, a survey of the rocky road that led to the 1944 accomplishment will be useful in understanding the arguments raised for and against proposed changes.

INTERNATIONAL MONETARY RELATIONS PRIOR TO WORLD WAR I

The history that led to Bretton Woods began with the international monetary system to which nations became accustomed in the thirty-five years before World War I. Britain was the leading trading nation and London the world financial center by the middle of the nineteenth century. The gold standard was firmly established in the British monetary system. By 1880 all of the major trading nations, and many lesser nations, were on gold or their currencies were related to gold. Under Britain's leadership international monetary relationships were to a high degree free of the exchange controls, devaluations, and withdrawals from gold that hindered world trade in the 1920's and 1930's.[1] Automatic forces of adjustment operated on prices and incomes to a degree not approached before or since, forcing "corrections" of nations' external disequilibrium positions. Central banks practiced monetary policy with a consciousness of national interest, but the flows of gold and capital upon which the system depended were preserved.[2]

International Investment

International investment by Britain, France, and Germany--the "surplus" countries--was very large in the latter part of the nineteenth century. The proportion of their national saving invested abroad ranged from one-third to one-half. Capital markets handling extensive foreign lending operations developed in Paris and Berlin to challenge London, where foreign issues had been accommodated for a century. The bank rate, raised or lowered as required to restore external equilibrium, became the favored instrument of monetary policy in the leading central banks.[3] Thus, the Bank of England managed Britain's external position by increasing the bank rate in the event of sustained gold outflow to induce capital imports and stem the outflow. Conversely, decreasing the rate induced lending abroad, permitting the countries experiencing deficits on goods and services account to avoid disequilibrium. Stabilizing transfers of capital, chiefly from London, were the key to the gold standard system.

The Gold Standard to 1914

The experience of the major trading nations with exchange rates pegged to gold during the years that bridged the nineteenth and twentieth centuries made the gold standard an international institution. International bankers considered gold _the_ international money. The ease with which international trade could be carried on and the certainty of gold or gold-equivalent settlement of international accounts led to an unfortunate confusion of form with function. Obscured by the smoothly operating system, economic stagnation afflicted most countries during the years 1873-96. Moreover, the conditions on which successful functioning of the system depended were undergoing change. The balance of power that Britain had maintained by might and diplomacy since 1815 was upset by the rise in Europe of a Germany united and strong and a France recovered from revolution and defeat. New trading rivals, the United States and Japan, emerged in North America and Asia. Thus, the nineteenth century economic and political order was transformed to Britain's disadvantage.

The conditions that undergirded the gold standard system during its "golden years" are seldom appreciated for their uniqueness by international bankers and statesmen. Benefits not inherent in the system were attributed to it; it did not, for example, automatically correct disequilibrium by some wonderfully simple mechanism. Nor did governments submit stoically to the discipline of the gold standard, even during the period of its smoothest operation, 1880-1914.[4] The system required tacit acceptance of basic "rules of the game," and the growing inclination of the major trading nations to practice nationalist policies in the pre-World War I period tested this requirement severely. A painfully achieved understanding of the conflict between the rigidities required by the system as against the flexibility sought by nations in their economic policy making emerged from the interwar period and was carried into planning of the Bretton Woods system.

The nineteenth century has properly been called "Britain's Century" in recognition of her extraordinary achievements in trade and colonial economic development. For the United States the century had a quite different meaning; rather than to world trade and colonial development, the nation turned to the development of its own vast western expanse. Aided by a policy of non-interference in European affairs, by an orderly process for admitting newly developed territories into the union, and by immigration, the territory, population, and wealth of the original thirteen states multiplied many times by 1900. As might have been expected, the new nation had less interest in, and sympathy for, the free trade movement than the established European powers.

The United States in the Pre-1914 World Economic Order

The economic advantages that Britain obtained from empire trade were in the United States obtained from intranational trade. Crude materials and foodstuffs moved from the West and South to the industrial North in trade for manufactureds, unhindered by tariff barriers. Consequently, imports from abroad declined steadily in relation to national income. By 1914 the national output exceeded that of Britain, Germany, France, Austria-Hungary, and Italy combined.

U.S. Tariff Policy

Tariffs were imposed continuously by the United States from its founding in 1789, justified, depending upon the occasion, by need for revenue or protection from "unfair" foreign competition. Rates on dutiable merchandise increased steadily until a level of 62 percent was reached in 1830. A gradual decline in rates brought them to a level of 20 percent in 1860, but the revenue needs of the Civil War forced increases that brought rates to 47 percent in 1865. For fifty years thereafter rates hovered near the 40 percent level. By the turn of the century, tariffs were a fixture in American politics and figured prominently in the elections of 1888, 1892, and 1896. The most transparent arguments in defense of high duty levels were pressed by protectionists, especially that prosperity depended on high tariff duties. When tariff "reform" was ultimately achieved in 1913, the outbreak of war prevented reduction of rates. The anti-free-trade philosophy of the United States of course affected the commercial treaty terms it negotiated with other countries. From 1860, when Britain and France negotiated the Cobden-Chevalier Treaty, the "most favored nation" principle was the goal of commercial diplomacy among major trading nations; but the United States rejected unconditional acceptance of the principle until 1923.

International Investment

The United States ran a net debtor position on capital account prior to World War I. Foreign purchases of Federal, state and corporate (largely railroad) bonds provided essential sources of funds for capital investment. A small passive balance was struck for all transactions during the 1850-73 period and a small active balance during the period 1874-1914. World trade did not count heavily in the economic life of the United States. Beginning in 1914, however, the tide of events became such that the nation would not again have the option of turning its back on the rest of the world.

THE WAR AND ITS AFTERMATH

The world monetary system, that had survived growing nationalist tendencies among the great powers since the 1870's, succumbed to autarkical policies in 1914. World War I inaugurated a new concept of belligerency whose most significant feature was its greatly augmented material requirements. Productive power replaced military power as the pivotal factor in war and vastly increased the importance of war finance. National treasuries strained to fill their war chests by resort to taxation, domestic war loans, liquidation of international investments, and foreign borrowing. Most countries involved in the war suspended convertibility of their currencies into gold and resorted ultimately to inflationary finance.

The four-year-long war destroyed the pre-1914 bases of political and economic relations among nations. Animosities were fanned to high emotional pitch by propaganda, and early rapprochement was impossible. The economies of the belligerents experienced widely differing degrees of dislocation, which hindered resumption of trade. France had been the principal battleground and suffered extensive physical destruction. Britain lost her commercial preeminence and liquidated a substantial part of her overseas investments to pay for the war. A vanquished Germany faced the necessity of refurbishing depleted capital facilities under the weight of reparations that would be scaled to French demands for revanche. The United States emerged from its relatively brief involvement in the war with a strong economy and a creditor status vis-a-vis Europe. As a heritage of the war, international monetary relationships would remain unsettled until the eve of World War II.

The Interwar Years

Cessation of hostilities did not restore prewar conditions to Europe. Social and political upheavals plagued many countries, especially in Eastern Europe. Hyperinflations occurred in Germany, Austria, Hungary, Russia and Poland during the five years following the Armistice.

Western Europe (outside of Germany) did not experience the social and political instability that afflicted the former imperial powers and the newly created Eastern European states. The stark lessons of international monetary policy recalled later at Bretton Woods were, nonetheless, learned from the shortsighted policies pursued during the interwar years by the United States, Britain and France.

Anticipation of Normal Exchange Rates, 1918-22

The institutional status of the gold standard is demonstrated by the speculative behavior of British and American investors who purchased depreciated European currencies in anticipation of their appreciation with the return of normal (gold) values. Stabilizing capital flows of this kind slowed temporarily the falling levels of some currencies, but continued depreciation of the currencies excited a sell-off and repatriation that seriously aggravated the pressure on them. The affected nations then resorted to devaluation to stem the outflow of gold. It was several years before restoration of gold convertibility was feasible. Britain went back on gold in 1925.

A unique factor in world monetary relations from the end of the war until the 1930's was the role of German reparations and their relationship to inter-allied war debts. Precedent for imposition of reparations on Germany after World War I was the imposition by Germany of reparations on France after the Franco-Prussian War. Conditions in the 1870's permitted relatively easy discharge of the French reparations levy; unfortunately, conditions did not favor discharge of the levy placed on Germany after 1918, an amount fixed in 1921 at $32 billion. Whatever may be said of Germany's willingness to pay the huge debt, the leading powers did not adjust their external policies to ease the burden of payment. Fiscal and monetary policy actions produced a recession in the United States during 1921-22, with resulting decreased imports. This was followed by imposition of higher U.S. tariffs in 1922. France, for its part, took advantage of a technicality in the reparations procedures to have Germany declared in default in 1921--before the amount of the reparations had even been established--and additional German territory on the east bank of the Rhine was occupied.

Unable to export and harassed by outflow of capital seeking a haven in foreign securities, Germany resorted to paper money. Every issue of paper money further reduced the value of the mark until Germany was no longer able to meet reparations. French occupation of the Ruhr followed. A trillion-fold inflation of the mark by 1923 then set the stage for German stabilization in 1924.

German reparations obligations and repayment to the United States of more than $10 billion in loans made to the Allied nations, the inter-Allied war debts, were considered related issues by Britain and France; only when Germany paid reparations did Britain and France pay their debts to the United States. Germany's ultimate default halted repayment of most inter-Allied debts. This experience caused the United States in 1934 to close its capital markets to flotation of issues by defaulted nations and, during the early World War II years, to insist on cash-basis sales to the Allied nations. Later, this policy was modified so that loans were made in return for lease of bases.

Stabilization, 1922-28

It was the confident expectation of statesmen and international bankers that normal international monetary relations would be restored after the war by a return to the gold standard. International conferences were convened at Brussels in 1920 and Genoa in 1922, to lay plans for gold restoration. The Genoa Conference, recognizing the disruption of prewar trade relationships and domestic equilibrium in many countries that had been wrought since 1914, urged a return to gold, but under conditions different from the prewar system. Central banks would play a more active role in international monetary affairs than before the war, carrying out activities such as absorbing and releasing gold to stabilize commodity prices.

In the period 1924-28, most countries returned to gold; Britain's restoration of gold in 1925 was a landmark event because the unfortunate parity chosen for the pound was the 1913 ratio. Prices in Britain had more than doubled during the war, hence the old parity became a strain on her commerce and could not be supported. Inflation had been much more serious in continental European countries, but they generally discounted the decline in purchasing power of their currencies when they restored gold parities. France stabilized in 1926 and, characteristically, undervalued the franc, an action that stimulated French exports and resulted in a large accumulation of gold reserves. French prosperity was matched by British recession as Britain sought to make the pound viable at the prewar parity by following deflationary policies in the domestic economy. For her efforts she reaped only labor strife. Germany, after stabilizing the mark in 1924, enjoyed a good credit rating in world capital markets and was able to meet her international obligations so long as capital movements supplied foreign exchange. Because the mark depended on uncertain capital movements, its stability was precarious.

Many countries elected to go on a gold-exchange standard, an adaptation to the general scarcity of gold nearly universal outside of the United States. A part of these countries' monetary reserves was held in gold and the remainder in short-term asset balances in New York or London. Gold coins were removed from circulation, except in the United States. The impact of international gold movements on domestic money supplies was increasingly managed by central banks, a policy that had been recommended by the Genoa Conference. "Sterilization" of gold by the central banks became a common practice. This was accomplished by absorbing or releasing gold, often through a stabilization fund, as required to stabilize commodity prices. All such policies had as their goal insulation of the domestic economy from international disturbances, and they reflect the increased importance countries attached by the mid-1920's to internal equilibrium vis-a-vis other goals.

Although the "rules of the game" that applied to the gold standard[5] were no longer observed, even in the pro forma prewar sense, the international monetary system appeared to be working smoothly by 1928. The system was, however, highly vulnerable to panic scrambles for gold by countries seeking safety from declining exchange positions of other countries, whose currency they held, out of fear that a weak exchange position might force suspension of gold payments. No action could more surely have brought about the feared suspension than competitive efforts to convert the suspect claims into gold. The gold-exchange standard system possessed an inherent deflationary bias[6] that was to upset the hopes of those who, encouraged by the apparent stability of the late 1920's, expected the system to muddle through. Violent political changes shook Europe and Asia during the 1930's and, against a setting of widespread economic depression, world monetary relations disintegrated into chaos.

The Depression Years: Failure of the Gold-Exchange Standard System

The gold-exchange standard system was doomed to failure from the start, as hindsight reveals with its typical crystal clarity. Each nation assumed a sovereign right to determine its exchange valuation and to convert its claims on foreigners into gold unilaterally and at its own pleasure. There was no general appreciation of how different the pre-1914 gold standard and the substitute gold-exchange standard were.[7] Similarities in form invited mistaken assumptions about similarities in function. Actually, a dangerous vacuum had been created; the adjustive mechanisms of the old standard--money supplies, prices, and incomes--ceased to operate with the same relentlessness under the new standard to correct disequilibria. The industrialized nations attempted to insulate their economies from the rest of the world by various neutralizing policies--sterilizing gold, restricting commodity output, and subsidizing prices--removing the necessity for their goods and services to meet the tests of international competition. Failure of the gold-exchange standard system in the 1930's can be laid to the failure of major countries to appreciate the degree of their monetary interdependence and the necessity for cooperation that it implied.

The appearance of relatively smooth operation in the international monetary system during the 1920's was produced by the saving factor of international investment. International capital transfers lacked the magnitude and the steadiness that characterized the prewar period, but international lending in London and New York enabled the system to work and, at the same time, concealed fundamental problems. A vulnerable structure of claims was built up that would collapse under the stress of economic contraction.

United States Foreign Investment. The United States was an unseasoned participant in long-term international lending compared to Britain and France. As a consequence of increased lending activities during the war, however, the United States emerged as Europe's creditor. It had been the practice for the United States to offset an active balance with Europe by remission of service charges and amortization on its European indebtedness. After the war, when the active balance with Europe increased, the United States reacted appropriately and lent long-term to Europe.

Throughout the 1920's, the United States invested large amounts of capital abroad. Movements of long-term capital (net) totaled $6.5 billion and short-term capital (net) $0.6 billion. Table 1 shows the detail of these capital movements and the net balance of the United States on goods and services, unilateral transfers, and gold. In each of the years 1919 to 1930, except 1922, 1926, and 1927, the United States maintained an active balance on All Transactions; only in those three years were long-term capital movements and unilateral transfers sufficient to offset surpluses on goods and services account. The large United States gold stock increased by $1.6 billion, 1919 to 1930, almost entirely from gold imports. Net gold exports occurred in only two of the eleven years. United States capital movements during these years were, in general, equilibrating; but the decade of the 1930's, under the stress of economic and political uncertainties, brought unstabilizing capital movements in great volume.

TABLE 1

INTERNATIONAL TRANSACTIONS OF THE UNITED STATES, 1919-39
(Millions of Dollars)

Year	Excess Receipts (+) Or Payments (-)			Net Inflow (+) Or Outflow (-) of Funds On Gold And Short-term Capital Account				Errors and Omissions[2]
	Net, Current and Long-term Capital Transactions	Net, Goods and Services and Unilateral Transfers	Long-term Capital[1]	Net Total	Changes In Monetary Gold Stock [Increase (-)]	Net Movement of- U. S. Short-term Capital	Net Movement of- Foreign Short-term Capital	
1939	+ 901	+ 888	+ 13	-1,689	-3,174	+226	+1,259	+ 788
1938	+1,197	+1,109	+ 88	-1,455	-1,799	+ 36	+ 317	+ 258
1937	+ 585	+ 62	+ 523	-1,008	-1,364	+ 43	+ 311	+ 423
1936	+ 657	- 93	+ 780	- 841	-1,272	+ 52	+ 376	+ 154
1935	+ 385	- 54	+ 437	- 750	-1,822	+427	+ 648	+ 365
1934	+ 624	+ 429	[3]+ 195	-1,044	-1,266	+104	+ 126	+ 420
1933	+ 220	+ 150	[3]+ 70	- 288	+ 131	+ 42	- 454	+ 68
1932	+ 420	+ 169	+ 251	- 499	- 53	+227	- 673	+ 79
1931	+ 405	+ 197	+ 208	- 504	+ 133	+628	-1,265	+ 99
1930	+ 469	+ 690	- 221	- 789	- 310	-191	- 288	+ 320
1929	+ 531	+ 771	- 240	- 147	- 143	-200	+ 196	- 384
1928	+ 214	+1,012	- 798	- 110	+ 238	-231	- 117	- 104
1927	- 275	+ 716	- 991	+ 698	+ 113	-349	+ 934	- 423
1926	- 251	+ 445	- 696	+ 326	- 93	- 36	+ 455	- 75
1925	+ 141	+ 684	[4]- 543	- 6	+ 100	- 46	- 60	- 135
1924	+ 315	+ 987	[4]- 672	- 137	- 256	-109	+ 228	- 178
1923	+ 522	+ 477	[4]+ 45	- 348	- 315	- 82	+ 49	- 175
1922	- 139	+ 645	- 784	- 269	- 269	NA	NA	+ 408
1921	+1,051	+1,613	- 562	- 735	- 735	NA	NA	- 216
1920	+1,837	+2,844	-1,007	+ 68	+ 68	NA	NA	-1,905
1919	+1,112	+3,824	-2,712	+ 166	+ 166	NA	NA	-1,278

Source: U.S. Bureau of Census, Historical Statistics of the United States, Colonial Times to 1957 (Washington,D.C.: 1960) p.464.

[1]Includes reinvested earnings of subsidiaries for 1919-1929.

[2]Includes, for 1919-39, certain adjustments to merchandise transactions and long-term capital

[3]1933 includes a net outflow of $40 million and 1934 a net inflow of $30 million of funds through arbitrage operation in securities which cannot be divided between domestic and foreign securities.

[4]Includes transactions in securities in 1923-25 which cannot be separated between domestic and foreign securities.

The Onset of Depression. The economic downturn that began in the United States in mid-1929 did not reveal itself initially as a cumulative contraction that would engulf most of the world for a full decade and earn the designation, "the Great Depression." Contractions of mild severity and brief duration had afflicted the economy in 1920-21, 1923-24, and 1926-27. There was, at the outset, reason to expect that the latest contraction would be of similar type. The explanation of the severity of the contraction and the spread of its contagion to other nations is still being debated.[8] It will be sufficient for present purposes to cite the impact of the contraction on the fragile world monetary system.

The international effect of the depression was transmitted primarily through reduced United States imports and reversal of its capital outflows. From 1929 to 1932, United States imports declined 35 percent by volume (60 percent by value) and long-term capital investment declined from a net outflow of $598 million to a net inflow of $277 million.[9] The countries that suffered these cutbacks were forced to restrict imports and pursue deflationary policies to encourage exports. Commodity-producing countries, especially, were disadvantaged by the depression. The failure of agriculture in the United States to adjust to reduced postwar demand levels had contributed to a general decline of commodity prices. Many commodity-producing countries were forced to borrow in the United States in order to offset their passive trade balances. Further reduction of their exports aggravated these countries' balance of payments positions and jeopardized their ability to service foreign debts. A further ramification of the decline in commodity-producing countries' exports was reduction of a source of dollars for Europe, dollars resulting from triangular trade. United States imports of primary commodities such as rubber, copper, tin, tea, silk, and coffee were supplied by countries with some of which Europe maintained an active balance and earned dollars.

The combination of United States tariff restrictions, reduced import demand, and reversal of capital outflow had profound effects on international trade. Between 1929 and 1932, the dollar value of world trade declined 60 percent. The truly international character of the depression is indicated by the pattern of trade reduction after 1929. Low-cost countries, that might have expected export gains, and high-cost countries, that might have expected import increases, suffered declining exports and imports.[10] The erosion of reserve positions, especially among the commodity-producing countries, was rapid.[11]

Withdrawal from Gold. The demand for liquidity by countries forced to meet passive balances in the period after 1929 revealed the weaknesses of the fixed-peg gold-exchange standard. An insufficient world gold supply, aggravated by accumulation of large gold reserves by the United States and France, augured ill for the survival of the system. A large volume of sensitive convertible claims, in the form of official bank deposits and currency, were on deposit in New York, London, and other financial centers. The mobility of these funds had been revealed during the speculative boom in the United States stock market and the ensuing crash. Speculative and precautionary motives excited their transfer.

Inadequate reserves forced some countries off gold and others to impose direct controls on their foreign exchange and imports. The United States and Western Europe clung to the gold standard together until 1931. In that year the failure of two large European banks, the Rothschild family's Kredit-Anstalt in Austria and the Darmstädter und National Bank in Germany, despite the intervention of major central banks with credits, triggered international transfers of liquid funds. As central banks moved to increase discount rates and attract funds, foreigners withdrew them--assuming their fears for the stability of the currency had been confirmed. Thus, in July, 1931, the mark was the victim of a run by foreigners and Germans alike. The pound, under almost continuous pressure as a consequence of Britain's weak balance of payments position, withstood threatening runs temporarily with the aid of foreign bank loans, then succumbed to sterling claims thrown on the New York market by the French. By the end of 1931, at least twenty countries had left the gold standard. The United States, France, the Netherlands, Belgium, and Switzerland attempted to maintain the gold standard with domestic reserves.

In the United States a substantial flight of capital occurred after Britain left the gold standard. Foreigners liquidated $1.3 billion of short-term assets in the United States in 1931; but the impact was partially offset by liquidation of $628 million of U.S. short-term assets abroad. Foreign short-term capital outflow from the United States continued in diminished amounts, of $673 million and $454 million in 1932 and 1933, and small net gold outflows occurred in 1931 and 1933. These movements reflected expectations that the dollar would be depreciated. By a series of Executive orders and Congressional legislation during 1933 the gold value of the dollar was reduced 41 percent and trade in gold was reserved exclusively to the United States Treasury. With the dollar undervalued in relation to European gold-bloc currencies, and a threatening political atmosphere developing, gold and capital moved to the United States in increasing volume. Table 1 gives the detail of the $10.7 billion gold inflow and $6.1 billion net long-term and short-term capital inflow that occurred from 1933 to 1939. The gold-bloc countries could not sustain indefinitely the outflow of gold and capital attracted by the undervalued dollar. When France devalued in 1936, the havoc wrought on the international monetary system by the Great Depression had run its course.

An opportunity to develop means of international monetary cooperation was forfeited in 1933 when the sixty-four nation London Economic Conference broke up, its expectations of cooperation in establishing new gold parities for major currencies dashed by an artless communication from President Roosevelt.[12] In the post-conference years the pound fluctuated freely for six years and the dollar for a year. A bloc of nations including British dominions and former colonies, Portugal, and the Scandinavian countries formed the sterling area and continued to keep reserve funds in London. The United States and the European gold-bloc countries maintained the ties to gold until 1936. Among the remaining major countries, i.e., the Fascist countries, Russia, China and Japan, some maintained a tenuous attachment to sterling and all employed direct controls. The three years after 1933 brought the low point of international monetary cooperation with repetitive devaluations, trade-reducing direct controls, and other manifestations of economic nationalism.

The Tripartite Agreement

The occasion of French devaluation in 1936 was preceded by efforts of Britain and the United States to secure a working agreement that would attempt to control retaliatory depreciation. If the pound, the dollar, and the franc could be stabilized, the problem of general exchange stability would be settled, since most countries were aligned with the pound or the dollar. An agreement was concluded by the three countries to consult on future exchange-rate changes, avoid competitive depreciation, and employ monetary policy to smooth exchange rate fluctuations. Other countries--the remaining members of the former gold-bloc, Italy, and Brazil--also abided by the agreement. A tenuous day-to-day stabilization among the dollar, pound, and franc was thus maintained until 1939, and large fluctuations in the value of the franc and the pound were accommodated within the agreement. The beginning of World War II cut off further experience under this cooperative endeavor.

The interwar years left a heritage of painfully acquired lessons to the planners of the post-World War II international monetary system. By 1942, British and American plans were being formulated for a system that would avoid both the rigidities of the gold standard and the frailties of the gold-exchange standard. The logic and substance of those plans that lay behind the compromise Bretton Woods agreement of 1944 will be discussed in the following chapter. A summary of the lessons taught in the interwar years follows.

LESSONS FOR BRETTON WOODS[13]

First Lesson

The first lesson that the postwar planners had to grasp was the danger of relying on speculative private capital to furnish funds for reconstruction after the war. Funds supplied by the American and British investors in the 1918-22 period were committed on naive assumptions and, when it was realized that normal currency values would not soon be restored, withdrawn summarily. As a consequence of speculative capital movements the weakness of many currencies was at first concealed, giving rise to underestimation of the degree of disequilibrium that actually existed, then revealed, inducing overestimation of the actual disequilibrium. Some alternative for sharing reconstruction costs among nations should wisely be substituted for private funds, and speculative capital movements should be subject to control.

Second Lesson

It was obvious from the post-1918 efforts of nations to stabilize their currencies in terms of gold that such actions should not be undertaken too soon after war, and that stabilization could not be undertaken unilaterally. Britain's experience with an overvalued pound, made worse by undervaluation of the franc, is the relevant example of what lies in the wake of unilateral stabilization. The period 1922-28 also made clear that gold parities are no panacea for correction of underlying disturbances. Par values of currencies should be fixed (cooperatively) in relation to existing general price levels. Moreover, as price levels change, international machinery should be available to facilitate changes in par values.

Third Lesson

It became clear in the years after 1930 that unemployment and price-flexibility could coexist, classical economic theory to the contrary. The rules of the gold standard game had lost their relevance in a world stricken by cumulative contraction. The domestic economy, under these circumstances, must be insulated from external transactions that will exacerbate depressed money and income flows, especially interest rate changes. Doubts about the beneficence of fluctuating exchange rates as a means to achieve independence of domestic from international money and income flows seemed confirmed by the interwar experience of Britain (1931-39) and the United States (1933-34). Some alternative between fixed-peg and "no peg" currencies had to be found.

Fourth Lesson

The shortage of liquidity available to countries that required it to meet temporary imbalances became clear when the United States reduced its imports after the onset of depression in 1929. Provision for lending foreign exchange to countries with temporary needs would have to be made to keep the postwar monetary system viable. Moreover, international sources of development loans would have to be provided to commodity-producing countries to reduce the degree of their vulnerability to contractions in the industrial countries.

Notes to Chapter 2

1. Arthur I. Bloomfield, _Monetary Policy Under the International Gold Standard, 1880-1914_ (New York: Federal Reserve Bank of New York, 1959), p.3.

2. _Ibid_., pp.23-26.

3. _Ibid_.

4. _Ibid_., pp.52-54; and, Oskar Morgenstern, _International Financial Transactions and Business Cycles_ (Princeton: Princeton University Press, 1959), p.441.

5. Bloomfield, _op. cit._, p.55

6. E. M. Bernstein, _International Effects of U.S. Economic Policy, Study Paper No. 16_ (Washington: Joint Economic Committee, 1960), p.8n.

7. Arthur D. Gayer, _Monetary Policy and Economic Stabilization_ (2nd ed.; New York: Macmillan, 1937), pp.44-45.

8. The most recent of the controversial inquiries into the causes of the recession is Milton Friedman and Anna Jacobson Schwartz, _A Monetary History of the United States, 1867-1960_ (Princeton: Princeton University Press, 1963).

9. Import data from John H. Adler, Eugene R. Schlesinger, and Evelyn Van Westerborg, _The Pattern of United States Import Trade Since 1923_ (New York:

Federal Reserve Bank of New York), pp.80, 82. On the general question of the international monetary effects of U.S. depression see Ragnar Nurkse, International Currency Experience (Princeton: League of Nations, 1944), and Arthur I. Bloomfield, Capital Imports and the American Balance of Payments, 1934-39 (Chicago: University of Chicago Press, 1950).

10. Robert Triffin, "National Central Banking and the International Economy," Lloyd A. Metzler, Robert Triffin and Gottfried Haberler, International Monetary Policies (Washington: Board of Governors of the Federal Reserve System, 1947), p.56.

11. Ibid. Triffin cites the loss by Colombia of 80 percent of its central bank gold and foreign exchange reserves between 1929 and 1931.

12. This is not to deny the high probability of conference failure from its beginning, given the deep disagreements among the major countries.

13. This section is based in large part on Eli Shapiro and Ezra Solomon, "International Monetary Relations," The Southern Economic Journal, January, 1950, pp. 310-25.

CHAPTER 3 DEVELOPMENT OF THE BRETTON WOODS SYSTEM

PLANNING THE POSTWAR INTERNATIONAL MONETARY SYSTEM

World War I and World War II: Comparisons

The apparent similarities between the two world wars--dependence of countries allied with the U.S. on its production of war materiel, delayed entry of the U.S. into the war, and preservation of the North American continent from physical destruction--obscure differences that, from the standpoint of international monetary affairs, were of great significance. World War II lasted two years longer and its burden in real and financial terms was several times greater than World War I; hence, relief and reconstruction needs were of much greater magnitude in 1945 than in 1919, and required an approach different from the ad hoc lending that sufficed in the post-World War I period.[1] World War II commenced during a recovery from the world-wide depression of the 1930's, in contrast to the relatively high level of economic activity in the years leading down to 1914. One consequence of this difference was that the economic dislocations of World War II were heaped upon a world economy already ridden by the disparities caused by depression. The economic disparities between the primary producing countries and the industrially developed countries were, therefore, greater in 1945 than in 1919.

Price disparities among countries, however, were generally less serious after World War II. A relative few countries experienced runaway inflation during World War II or its aftermath. This was partly attributable to the slack that existed in the economies of most countries when the war commenced, but also to the practice in many countries of imposing financial controls--internal and external--insulating their economies from demand-pull pressures, and to the reduced necessity for deficit financing by governments that benefited from Lend-Lease aid. Foreign exchange holdings of the United Nations were larger in 1945 than they had been in 1939, chiefly because of Lend-Lease aid.[2]

Finally, problems that plagued international relations in the post-World War I period--reparations payments and inter-Allied war-debts--were of secondary importance after World War II. A lesson had been learned from the interwar period.

An extraordinary integration of resource planning was achieved by the United Nations in their drive to victory--a state of cooperation that barely survived the war. Nonetheless, the means were provided for the United Nations to counsel and develop machinery for meeting postwar problems. International monetary problems occupied an important place in the agenda.

The Bretton Woods Agreement

Several months before the U.S. became a belligerent, an American-British declaration,[3] the Atlantic Charter, proclaimed, among other objectives, the broad measures of economic cooperation that would be sought after the war. The declaration reflected a conclusion that the spirit in which international economic relations had been conducted in the interwar years had to share some of the blame for World War II. Moreover, the aggravated problems of those years--undervaluation and overvaluation of currencies, competitive devaluation, failure to service debts, and insufficient and maldistributed liquidity--all had their origin in nationalistic policy making and inadequate planning.

The first tangible step to avoid the mistakes of the past developed from the American-British Lend-Lease aid agreement of 1941. In order that postwar planning not be handicapped with war-debt problems, it was implied that Britain could expect a generous settlement of claims arising out of Lend-Lease. A reciprocal action by Britain was that she pledge herself to cooperate with the United States in securing reduction of trade barriers and removal of preferential tariff duties.[4] Thus, the U.S. began constructive planning for its postwar creditor role, a role that would inevitably be far greater than ever before.

The discussions between American and British representatives concerning the disposition of Lend-Lease claims against Britain inaugurated a forum that continued throughout the war years. Immediate postwar problems, such as the need for relief and reconstruction aid to countries that had been occupied by the enemy, were discussed during 1941-42 and culminated in the organization of the United Nations Relief and Rehabilitation Administration in 1943. Similar discussions preceded the proposals for an International Monetary Fund and an International Bank for Reconstruction and Development in 1944 by the Bretton Woods United Nations Monetary and Financial Conference, and the proposal to form a permanent international organization, the United Nations, by the Dumbarton Oaks Conference the same year. Thus, the problems that would confront the world immediately after cessation of hostilities and over the long term were anticipated well in advance of the war's end, and machinery proposed to meet them. We shall see later that the problems of the transition period, between UNRRA and the effective mounting of the IMF and IBRD, were not anticipated in the wartime discussions among the United Nations.

There was encouraging evidence a full year before the war ended that some of the lessons of the interwar years were being heeded, and the United Nations were taking advantage of their wartime coalition to develop new remedies for old problems. Relief and reconstruction needs would be met by international organizations rather than be dependent on private capital flows as in 1919. Discussion of Lend-Lease claims indicated that war-debts might not threaten the spirit of co-operation generated among the United Nations during war. Exchange stability and loans for development would, one might hope, have a future under the proposed IMF and IBRD different from the interwar history. These new financial institutions were regarded, especially in the United States, as pivotal in postwar planning. Their origin in American-British discussions, and the rationale for their structure and proposed functions, were important factors in postwar international monetary developments.

The Keynes Plan and the White Plan: Formulas for Bretton Woods

The condition for which the United States was willing to hold open its claims on Britain for Lend-Lease aid, noted above, was a pledge of British cooperation with the United States in matters of postwar international economic policy. This requirement was formalized in the much discussed Article VII of the 1941 Lend-Lease agreement. Discussion of the areas of cooperation that might be implied in this agreement concerned the British, who, from the early days of the war, had no illusions about the problems they would face after the war with respect to exports. According to Professor Penrose, the measures on which cooperation was implied by Britain's acceptance of Article VII were determined, after joint discussion, to include:[5]

1. An international organization for the maintenance of exchange stability and to deal with balance of payments problems in member countries;
2. An international organization to deal with long-term international investment;
3. An international agreement on primary commodity price control;
4. International measures for the reduction of trade barriers;
5. The international organization of relief and reconstruction; and,
6. Measures to maintain full employment.

In these points is reflected a desire to anticipate and, if possible, avoid some problems that proved upsetting in the interwar years. Internationalization of efforts to promote exchange stabilization and long-term investment, providing aid for relief and reconstruction, and reduction of trade barriers--points number 1, 2, 4 and 5--in particular reflect a desire to avoid anguish that resulted from nationalistic economic policies that arose after World War I. Point number 3, an international agreement on primary commodity price control, reflects concern for the nonindustrial countries, whose well-being swung violently with the economic cycle of the industrialized countries during the interwar period. Point number 6, the necessity of measures to maintain full employment, deserves comment because of its novelty vis-a-vis the post-World War I era.

During the years immediately prior to World War II, many industrial economies began to practice internal, as well as external, policies to stimulate their domestic economies. The classical (in Keynes' sense) economics joined the gold standard values in having lost its authority. Britain's recovery after leaving the gold standard in 1931, and the rarity of her relative prosperity in the midst of world depression, were events with great significance to economists around the world. Moreover, the Keynesian rationale for making full employment a primary objective of government policy had gained a large following in Britain and elsewhere. Britain, as expected, pressed the issue of full employment in postwar economic planning. The importance that inheres in mixing the full employment objective with international monetary questions should be understood; basically, it affected each of the other measures called for by Article VII. An international monetary system would have to be designed to provide for adjustive mechanisms that would replace the classical wage and price mechanisms under fixed exchange rates. The way was open for an extraordinary innovation in the international monetary system, and the earliest outline of the nature and scope of a postwar system was developed by John Maynard Keynes, drawing on his long period of concern with international monetary reform.

The Keynes Plan. Keynes had been an adviser to the British Treasury since the early years of World War I, and all of Britain's economic planning for the post-World War II era bears in some degree the imprint of his thought. By 1923, Keynes had described the deflationary biases of the gold standard and argued the case for the gold exchange standard,[6] and by 1933, in anticipation of the London Economic Conference, he had conceived the broad outlines of an international organization, a world central bank, that would have functions somewhat similar to those assigned a decade later to the International Monetary Fund.[7] With the publication of _How to Pay for the War_, Keynes became deeply involved in wartime economic policy and, in June, 1940, moved into the British Treasury--as a private citizen without civil service status and unsalaried.[8] From Lend-Lease, through Bretton Woods and the postwar British loan, Keynes was intimately involved with formulation of British economic policy.

Keynes was apprehensive from the beginning of the war that Britain's ability to cover her large merchandise account deficit might be lost by the drain of war, forcing her to resort to autarkical policies. Article VII was viewed by the Prime Minister, and many of the Whitehall official family, as an encumberment, chargeable to American naiveté, of Britain's capacity to survive after the war. The problems that Britain would face on the balance of payments front were little understood for their true gravity on this side of the Atlantic. Article VII was, for President Roosevelt, the object of a political trade by which the U.S. Senate was appeased for extending aid to a belligerent while the United States remained a "neutral" bystander; for the Secretary of State, Cordell Hull, however, Article VII was the vindication of a career interest with free trade in which multilateralism approached the status of a fetish. The Secretary's intent was clear; the leverage afforded by the Lend-Lease agreement would be used to extract a British concession on empire preference.[9] Internationalism appealed basically to the inclinations of the British, whose policies down to World War II compared favorably, to say the least, with the protectionist leanings of the United States. Despite a substantial sentiment at Whitehall favoring the U.S. position on Article VII, the practical matter for the British was to anticipate the problem of reviving export trade under awesome handicaps--physical reconstruction requirements, neglected foreign markets, liquidated overseas investments, and accumulated external debts.

As a British representative during discussions in Washington concerning Article VII, Keynes grasped fully the dilemma in which his country found itself. Characteristically, he bent himself to the task of devising a means by which the American view might be accommodated while, at the same time, securing British postwar interests.[10] Building on ideas that he had expounded for twenty-five years, Keynes developed his plan for an International Clearing Union.

If multilateralism were to rule post-World War II

international economic affairs, there would have to exist, beyond the American penchant for free flow of goods among nations, some system for clearing multilaterally the payments made by one nation to another. In Keynes' words, "The Principal object (of the International Clearing Union) can be explained in a single sentence: To provide that money earned by selling goods to one country can be spent on purchasing the products of any other country. In jargon, a system of multilateral clearing. In English, a universal currency valid for trade transactions in all the world. Everything else in the plan is ancillary to that."[11]

The gold standard, and the gold-exchange standard as it operated during the interwar years, both tended to have a deflationary bias, as explained in Chapter 2. Countries operating under the full gold standard were obliged by the "rules of the game" to reinforce the restrictive effects of gold outflows by appropriate policies such as high interest rates, and conversely with respect to gold inflows. Under the gold-exchange standard, after World War I, countries with strong net export balances--the United States and, after 1926, France--tended to hoard gold, inducing a contraction in effective demand for total imports. These and other shortcomings of interwar monetary relations among nations were cited by Keynes in a statement that set out the purpose of his plan:[12]

> We need an instrument of international currency having general acceptability between nations, so that blocked balances and bilateral clearings are unnecessary. . .
>
> We need an orderly and agreed method of determining the relative exchange values of national currency units, so that unilateral action and competitive exchange depreciations are prevented.
>
> We need a quantum of international currency, which is neither determined in an unpredictable and irrelevant manner as, for example, by the technical progress of the gold industry, nor subject to large variations depending on the gold reserve policies of

> individual countries; but is governed by the actual current requirements of world commerce, and is also capable of deliberate expansion and contraction to offset deflationary and inflationary tendencies in effective world demand.
>
> We need a system possessed of an internal stabilizing mechanism, by which pressure is exercised on any country whose balance of payments with the rest of the world is departing from equilibrium in either direction, so as to prevent movements which must create for its neighbours an equal but opposite want of balance.
>
> We need an agreed plan for starting off every country after the war with a stock of reserves appropriate to its importance in world commerce, so that without undue anxiety it can set its house in order during the transitional period to full peace-time conditions.
>
> We need a central institution, of a purely technical and nonpolitical character, to aid and support other international institutions concerned with the planning and regulation of the world's economic life.
>
> More generally, we need a means of reassurance to a troubled world, by which any country whose own affairs are conducted with due prudence is relieved of anxiety for causes which are not of its own making, concerning its ability to meet its international liabilities; and which will, therefore, make unnecessary those methods of restriction and discrimination which countries have adopted hitherto, not on their merits, but as measures of self-protection from disruptive outside forces.

Keynes' plan envisaged an international clearing system not unlike the clearing systems through which banks offset claims against each other in a domestic banking system. A country earning foreign exchange would be credited, in the union, with an equivalent amount of an internationally acceptable currency called bancor. The account would be credited or debited to settle sales or purchases in international trade. Balances not settled by offsetting one country's accounts against another would be cleared through the union.

To provide the initial balances necessary if countries were to ride out the postwar transition to normal trade relations, bancor credits would be extended through the operation of overdraft facilities of the kind found in British banking operations. The amount of credits available to any country would reflect its relative importance in prewar world trade. Total credits of $26 billion were suggested by Keynes.[13] In normal times, after the transition period, countries experiencing net debit accounts would be able to obtain bancor through automatic overdraft privileges with the Clearing Union. Every central bank would be obligated to accept bancor payments. Wide limits were suggested for overdrafts and positions in excess of the limits, either creditor or debtor, were to be penalized at a specified rate per annum. Creditor nations were expected to take action to reduce their creditor positions, and a suggestion for cancelling the credits of a country that accumulated bancor assets and refused to follow policies that would reduce them was favored by Keynes.

The Clearing Union, thus, had an inherent expansionist bias, in contrast to the contractionist bias of the gold standard. Hoarding of bancor by creditor countries was discouraged by the penalties, by the fact that credits could not be converted to gold (although the converse was possible), credits could not be held without incurring an interest "cost", and by threat of cancellation. Moreover, the credits initially provided would, in a world deprived of consumer and producer goods for more than six years, experience a rapid rate of turnover. The large reserves of liquidity provided to countries as a result of their drawing privileges would, in Keynes' view, enable a country to achieve internal and external equilibrium without resorting to exchange depreciation, exchange control, or bilateralism. Implicit in the plan was Keynes' assumption that a world in which full employment was generally achieved would have no reason to make recourse to exchange depreciation, because internal and external equilibrium rates would converge.[14]

The White Plan. The Keynes Plan was received in the United States in the summer of 1943, and an alternate American plan prepared by Harry Dexter White and his associates[15] in the U.S. Treasury Department was forwarded at the same time to the British. A prospectus of the White Plan, in the form of an early statement of its objectives comparable to Keynes' statement quoted above, revealed the role that White intended for his creation. The prospectus was entitled, "Suggested Plan for a United Nations Stabilization Fund and a Bank for Reconstruction of the United and Associated Nations." Gardner describes it as follows:[15]

> It aimed 'to prevent the disruption of foreign exchanges and the collapse of monetary and credit systems; to assure the restoration of foreign trade; and to supply the huge volume of capital that will be needed virtually throughout the world for reconstruction, for relief, and for economic recovery.' The two institutions whose creation was proposed were designed 'to carry on effective work as soon as the war is over. It would be ill-advised, if not possibly dangerous, to leave ourselves at the end of the war unprepared for the stupendous task of world-wide economic reconstruction.'

Considering the historic isolation of the United States, Roosevelt's attitude toward international monetary cooperation at the time of the London Economic Conference, and the unequalled self-sufficiency of the United States, the early drafts of the White Plan were bold beyond anyone's expectations. Two new institutions, the Fund and the Bank, were to be the chief agencies in postwar international finance. They were to have a sovereignty of their own and function without regard to national political considerations. The Stabilization Fund, capitalized at $5 billion or more in gold currency and government securities obtained from member countries (half to be subscribed immediately, half deferred), would make short-term loans to member countries in order that they might be able to ride out periods of temporary disequilibrium in their external positions. A quid pro quo was provided: In return for borrowing privileges, member countries would have to surrender control of their exchange rates, abolish exchange control, and submit to monitoring of their domestic policies by the Fund. The Bank, capitalized at $10 billion in gold and local currency obtained from member countries (half to be subscribed immediately and half deferred), was to be a true international bank and the supplier of capital for reconstruction, relief, and economic recovery needs resulting from the war. It would buy and sell gold and securities, discount bills, issue notes, and make long-term loans at low interest.[16] The implied objective--to shift the balance of international lending from private to international organization sources--was consistent with the expressed desires of the Secretary of the Treasury.[17]

A Plan for Bretton Woods. The Keynes and White plans were both shorn of some of their idealistic "excesses" before the British and American representatives began seriously to work out a compromise program for postwar international finance. All who participated in the final proposal understood that they would have to fashion a system that would be acceptable at home. This was a more demanding constraint on the American than the British side, the U.S. Senate having begun, after the 1942 elections, to revert to type--with conservative sentiments making allies of Southern Democrats and Republicans, the alliance bent on obstructing any grandiose plans for reordering the affairs of men, international-economic or otherwise, through government.[18] Thus, the coat was cut to fit the cloth, and the White Plan suffered most through multiple revisions. In contrast to the early drafts, the final version of the White Plan had modified the bank's functions, and the bank was separated from the fund, in joint discussions until late 1943.

Both the Keynes and White plans provided against the failings of the old international monetary order--profiting from the "lessons of the interwar years" and building on the Tripartite Agreement. Exchange rates would not be unilaterally determined--an invitation to profitless circular retaliation as during the 1930's--but would instead be controlled by an international agency. To facilitate exchange stability, supplemental sources of liquidity would be provided, thus compensating for possible hoarding of gold by creditor countries. Countries would no longer be required to settle their debtor positions through direct trade or borrowings from their creditors--Europe's predicament during the depression when triangular trade ceased to supply dollars--but, through a system of multilateral clearing, would achieve equilibrium by means of earnings in multilateral trade. Finally, the plans recognized that the international economic policies of member nations would have to be monitored lest they disrupt international equilibrium.

The differences between the plans concerned the nature of the liquidity fund and its size, the ease of access to the fund by debtor countries, the role assigned to gold, and other features of lesser importance. Keynes was for a new international monetary system with banking functions and a substantial pool of an international currency; White was for a deposit-created fund with limited functions and without the characteristics of a currency. Keynes would permit drawing privileges to be automatic and fix liberal drawing limits; White would restrict drawing rights with fixed limits related to a country's quota deposit. Keynes saw gold as the medium in terms of which bancor was defined and as an alternate form of liquidity; White provided for gold to be a part of the quota deposit, or a fully secured special deposit, and as a means for buying currencies that the fund might declare "scarce". In fundamental ways the two plans differed in structure and function, if not in objective.

Negotiations by the British and American representatives (including Canadian and French representatives) in 1943 led to an early decision to drop the Keynes Plan in favor of the Stabilization Fund. The choice was made on grounds of the more modest objectives, closer controls, and lesser expense to the United States of the Stabilization Fund. With the abandonment of their plan, the British pressed for changes of a liberalizing nature in the chosen plan, not without considerable success. The issues that divided the representatives were the size and availability of the fund's resources, the mechanisms of adjustment for maintaining equilibrium in the balance of payments, and the resources to be made available to ease the postwar transition to normal international financial relations.

The size of the fund was cut to about one-third the amount proposed by Keynes because an American contribution of $3 billion was represented as the maximum Congress would accept.[19] If the size of the fund was limited, then the overdraft principle was an impossible means for giving countries access to its resources. The British insisted that the resources of the fund, if they were to be so small, would have to be available to debtor countries on an automatic basis. Ultimately this view was compromised; the fund would remain a passive agency except in obvious cases of misuse of its resources.

The mechanisms-of-adjustment issue concerned exchange rate stability and flexibility, the role of the fund in monitoring a debtor country's domestic policies, and the penalties to be imposed on creditor countries that persisted in hoarding liquidity. To protect a country's efforts to achieve full employment, Keynes sought (reversing his own earlier position) to shift the adjustment process to exchange rates. Instead of a pegged rate, an adjustable pegged rate was introduced. Member countries might alter their exchange rate by any amount if required to correct a fundamental disequilibrium. For changes of less than 10 percent from the original par value, a country could proceed without fund approval regardless of the character of the domestic policies that may have induced the disequilibrium. Indeed the British succeeded, during the negotiations, in having retained the provision of the White Plan that permitted a determination by the fund of the appropriate economic policies that would have to be followed by members. Creditor countries, however, in the British view, should be subject to sanctions that would pressure them into halting hoarding practices. White's suggestion was a provision that would permit the fund to declare a currency "scarce" whenever it increased its fund credit beyond a stated amount, whereupon the fund's remaining holding of the currency would be rationed and debtor countries might discriminate against the creditor country's exports. Keynes regarded it as a safe bet that the United States, the probable creditor country for many years to come, would take action in advance of the dollar being declared scarce to insure that the action would never be necessary.

Finally, with regard to the resources required to ease the immediate postwar transition, the introduction of the White proposal for a reconstruction bank into negotiations a scant few weeks prior to the Bretton Woods meeting calmed British fears that the war's end would find a void in international financial planning. Despite the limited capitalization provided in the bank and its restriction to a cautious lending policy, it was a source of reconstruction finance that would help meet immediate needs. The commencement of the fund's operations, with its requirement for removal of exchange restrictions and other impediments to the free flow of trade and capital, threatened the British, who pressed for a period of grace before efforts to accomplish multilateralism would be expected. Transitional problems would, despite these moves, prove to have been unanticipated in their full complexity and burden; the planning for the immediate postwar period was wholly inadequate.

It required but three weeks for the Bretton Woods International Monetary and Financial Conference to frame Articles of Agreement for the International Monetary Fund and International Bank for Reconstruction and Development from the compromise plans worked out by British and American representatives.[20] Forty-four countries signed the Agreement. The objective of the Fund, stated in Article I, is "to shorten the duration and lessen the degree of disequilibrium in the international balance of payments of members." To accomplish this end the Articles charged the Fund: to promote international monetary cooperation through machinery for consultation and collaboration on international monetary problems; to facilitate the expansion and balanced growth of international trade and contribute thereby to the promotion and maintenance of high levels of employment and real income of all members; to promote exchange stability, maintain orderly exchange arrangements, and avoid competitive exchange depreciation; to assist in the establishment of a multilateral system of payments and the elimination of foreign exchange restrictions; and, to give confidence to members by making the Fund's resources available to them under adequate safeguards, thus providing them with the opportunity to correct maladjustments in their balance of payments without resorting to measures destructive of national or international property.

The Fund and Bank agreements were considerably more detailed than the joint statements from which they had sprung, because of legalistic specification of privileges and obligations. Basic to the International Monetary Fund agreement was the principle that a country's exchange rate should be stable except as it was demonstrated to be untenable by "fundamental disequilibrium" (not further defined) in the country's external accounts. When a fundamental disequilibrium was demonstrated, the member country could change its exchange rate up to 10 percent from the initial parity (described below) upon prior notification of the Fund, and the Fund could not object. For changes greater than 10 percent the Fund was given discretion. Drawing rights in the Fund were provided to enable a country to ride out temporary disequilibria. These drawing rights permitted a member country to purchase from the Fund, with its own currency, the currency of any other member up to a limit of 25 percent of its quota per year subject to another limit that restricted the Fund's holdings of the purchasing country's currency to not more than 200 percent of its quota. A member's quota normally was subscribed 25 percent in gold or dollars and 75 percent in its own currency.

Thus, a member country could purchase foreign exchange up to 125 percent of its quota. Drawings of 25 percent in successive years required the approval of the Fund's Board of Directors. The total Fund quota was to be $8 billion which placed an approximate limit on any single year's total draw of $1 billion.[21]

The Agreement made clear that a purchasing country was expected to repurchase its own currency. In any year in which such a country's international reserves increased, half the increase was to be applied to repurchases.[22] Additional inducements to repurchase were interest and service charges levied against the excess of Fund holdings of a country's currency and the country's quota. The problem of repurchase for a debtor country was complicated by the requirement that repurchases be paid for with gold or convertible currencies.

Whether the drawing rights of a country were automatic or conditional has been interpreted both ways. They were neither as automatic as the British would have preferred nor as conditional as the Americans would have preferred. The language of the agreement states that a member country "shall be entitled" to purchase currency provided the payments to be made in the borrowed currency are consistent with the provisions of the Fund Agreement. However, the British[23] objected that the qualifications on purchase of currency removed any pretense of automatic drawing rights, and the United States Senate was assured by its Bretton Woods principals, including White, that a member's right to purchase currency was conditional.[24]

Member nations bound themselves to establish a par value for their currencies in relation to the gold content of the U.S. dollar in 1944. Official Fund transactions between member countries are based on these par values and members are required to contain variations between spot prices and par values of member currencies in their foreign exchange markets to plus or minus 1 percent. Exchange rates under normal circumstances were fixed within this narrow margin.

The "scarce" currency provision, suggested by White, survived both the Bretton Woods Conference and the United States Senate. It constituted one of the few powers that the Fund might exercise over members, the others being denial of the resources of the Fund to a member not fulfilling the Fund purposes, requiring a member to consult with Fund officers, and waiving specified provisions of the Fund Agreement.

The Fund was inevitably fated to have a wide

influence as a center for consultation--between the Fund and members and among members--and to become important as a source of expert opinion, a publisher of international data, and a producer of research. In fact, during its first decade it was notable primarily for these "nonfinancial" activities.

It would seem justified, considering the preceding review of the Keynes and White plans in their original form and at their creative best, to conclude that the Bretton Woods accomplishment was an unimaginative and disappointing dilution of the brilliant proposals offered by Keynes and White in 1943.

The multilateral clearing machinery and the international currency had been stripped away and the ambitious plans to expand liquidity resources and fix equal responsibility on creditors and debtors to correct disequilibrium had been watered down. Perhaps, to have expected that every novel proposal would, solely on the strength of its ingenuity, find its way into the Agreement was to place too much reliance on the lofty principles that grew out of wartime unity and dedication. If anyone had reason to lament the Bretton Woods accomplishment, it would seem to have been Keynes. His ingenious proposals, some of which had been formulated over a period of many years, were for the most part rejected. But Harrod[25] assures us that Keynes departed the Conference with a high sense of gratification, confident that the Agreement was only a beginning.

In historical context the Bretton Woods Agreement was a highly significant accomplishment. An observer of the interwar years would, in 1944, have been justified in confidently predicting that international monetary cooperation could only fare better after World War II, and cause less disruption to both world trade and the stability of national economies, than during the post-World War I period. The principle was established that the burdens of international adjustment should no longer depend solely on national price and wage changes that had slavishly supported rigid exchange rates in the interwar years. Exchange rates would, henceforth be stable in the short run, aided where necessary by IMF resources, while in the long run they would be adjustable as required to correct structural differences that caused countries to suffer prolonged debtor positions. The International Monetary Fund would sit in judgment on exchange rate practices and monitor rate changes. With the means available for the adjustment of its exchange rate, a country would, it was reasoned, have less reason to take refuge behind restrictive exchange practices and other hindrances to multilateral trade. Freedom from exchange restrictions, a condition vigorously sought by the American delegation,[26] became a primary goal of the IMF in the early postwar period, and it could be a reasonable goal only under the adjustable peg system established at Bretton Woods.

A period of grace was provided in the Agreement in order that the transition from wartime currency controls to peacetime currency interconvertibility might be smoothed. Article XIV specified a five year period after the Fund began operation (March 1, 1947) during which the system of existing controls, imposed during the war or after the war by debtor countries to protect their scarce reserves, might be gradually removed. Beginning March 1, 1950, the Fund would require reports from member countries concerning the extent of their restrictions. Steadily increasing pressure would be imposed thereafter on discriminating countries, climaxing in the possible denial of eligibility to use the Funds resources.

Creditor countries acceded in the Agreement to the principle that they had a partial responsibility for correcting balance of payments disequilibrium. This admission proved to have great significance with respect to the United States, whose dollar aid was decisive in paving the way for reconstruction and economis revival in Europe and Asia. U.S. aid, IBRD loans, and (after convertibility was achieved in 1958) private investment far exceeded the loan and transfer volume that was assumed to be the postwar requirement.

Finally, the creation of a medium for consultation and to explore additional means to promote international monetary cooperation was an important accomplishment. It was expected that the IMF would tie in with other international economic programs, especially the proposed International Trade Organization. Events quickly proved that economic nationalism was still a powerful force, and that the IMF had no magic powers to dispel it. But the discourse begun out of necessity in the early 1940's between two countries continued among many countries--also out of necessity.

MOUNTING THE BRETTON WOODS SYSTEM

Ominous Beginnings

Many of the countries whose delegates had signed the Bretton Woods Agreement made more than a pro forma exercise of accepting membership in its two institutions. The efforts of the delegates to tailor the agreement to forms that would be politically acceptable in Washington and London, in the process emasculating features that had been considered vital in the Keynes and (early) White plans, proved, nonetheless, to have been overly optimistic. Within a year the spirit of the agreement was being challenged by nationalist impulses in both capitals. Senator Robert A. Taft led a last bastion fight to prevent his country's membership. The reaction was put down only after an almost unbelievable stretching by proponents of the accomplishments that might be expected from U.S. participation. Testimony by Administrative officials implied that acceptance of the Fund and Bank would obviate any necessity for additional U.S. financial participation in postwar reconstruction and recovery, would assure speedy removal of exchange controls by foreign countries (and protection under the proposed International Trade Organization against controls over transfer of goods), and that access to the Fund would--according to the American interpretation--be strictly conditional and limited.[27] In Britain the challenge to participation was no less pointed and it endured even after American acceptance was a fact. The Bank of England feared that the world financial center would shift from London to New York, and the newspapers warned against any reliance on American cooperation.[28] Other criticisms were that the Agreement would tie sterling too close to gold, jeopardize the system of imperial preference when it was most needed, and place a disproportionate burden on debtor, rather than creditor, countries to make adjustments in periods of disequilibrium.[29] The defense of the agreement by the Government involved fully as much wishful imagery as its American counterpart. Keynes implied to his critics that the drawing rights in the Fund would be automatic, and that the U.S. would be forced by the "scarce-currency" clause to relieve dollar scarcity in international finance.[30] Gardner's quotation from the Manchester Guardian sums up the British understanding of Bretton Woods participation:[31]

> We are free to maintain exchange control, free to do away with gold except as an accounting device, free to vary our exchange rate and free to discriminate against the goods of any country which is declared an under-importer.

Obviously, the wide variance that existed between the two most important participants in their official concepts of the nature and functions of the Bretton Woods institutions portended conflicts in getting them into operation. Nor were the remaining countries all enthusiastic about membership. Many smaller countries had depleted their gold and dollar reserves and considered the quota subscriptions a burden. However, a sufficient number of countries had accepted membership by the end of 1945 to mount the Fund and the Bank. On December 27, 1945, they were formally established, and at year-end the membership included thirty-five of the forty-four countries represented at Bretton Woods.

The Savannah Meeting

A joint meeting of the Fund and the Bank Boards of Directors was convened in Savannah on March 8, 1946, to settle myriad operational matters such as the permanent site of the twin institutions, operational procedures, and qualifications and salaries of the Executive Directors. The difficulties encountered by the Board members in resolving decisions about these "housekeeping requirements" augured ill for the future of international monetary cooperation under the Bretton Woods System. Differences of opinion that had been salved over during the 1944 Conference emerged at Savannah to split the meeting and kindle ill feeling. The United States, never having shared the British view that the Bretton Woods institutions should function in an international ether unspoiled by considerations of national sovereignty, mobilized its influence to achieve its will. Armed with the largest quota, hence the largest number of votes,[32] and with the Board members keenly aware that the dominant member was and would continue to be the world's leading creditor, the United States took a rigid position on the permanent site of the Fund and Bank (it would be in Washington), forced the issue on the political responsibilities of the Executive Directors (they would be full-time politically appointed national representatives), and contradicted the prevailing view of the British that the salaries of the Directors be modest (they would equal or exceed the highest civil service levels in most member countries).

Arrangements were made at Savannah to hold the first annual meeting of the IMF and IBRD on May 6 in Washington. The chief business transacted consisted in choosing the Managing Director, Camille Gutt, of Belgium.

By hindsight, the American view on the political character of the Fund proved realistic; not having been able to mount an international political organization that could operate above national sovereignty, the world could scarcely have expected an international economic organization so established to operate effectively. The site choice was probably unfortunate; but more lamentable was the forceful presentation of the American view with respect to this issue and others on the agenda. There was no apparent awareness among the American representatives that their attitude at Savannah vitiated the spirit of Bretton Woods and created distrust of American policies yet to come.

The Fund Gets Down to Business

Establishing Par Values for Member Currencies

The first official act to carry out the Fund provisions was the Directors' call for member countries to submit par values of their currencies. Within thirty days from September 12, 1946, each country was required by the Agreement to submit an initial par value based on exchange rates prevailing sixty days before the Agreement became official, i.e., rates prevailing on

October 28, 1945. Before the end of 1946 thirty-two countries had complied and their initial parities had been announced by the Fund. The Fund accepted the rates submitted in every case.

Some criticism was directed at the Fund for accepting member country par values without any adjustment. The Fund Agreement (Article XX) had specified that the rates prevailing sixty days before the Fund commenced operations should be accepted unless the member country or the Fund objected to the rate, in which case the rate should be negotiated. It was the Directors' judgment that, rather than attempt to anticipate the rate that would, over the long term, effect a balance between internal and external equilibrium for any particular member, they would accept the rate initially proffered and stand ready to employ the Fund's machinery to adjust it as required. The highly uncertain character of the immediate postwar economic environment was, therefore, the consideration on which the Directors decided to accept the rates as submitted.

The initial rates tended to overvalue member country currencies. Metzler[33] has shown, using prewar price index data for nineteen member countries, that the Fund rates exceeded purchasing-power parity rates in fourteen countries. Overvaluation was a rational policy to employ against inflation pressures, especially if removal of exchange controls was to weigh heavily among the Fund's short-term goals. Few countries were in any position to undertake export policies, to which an overvalued currency would be an impediment. Pending reconstruction and economic recovery, selective imports were desperately needed and they could best be obtained with a combination of overvalued currency and direct controls. Significantly, Britain and some of the dominions undervalued their currencies. This policy apparently was based on a belief that recovery of an export capability was vital to Britain's survival, and that inflation in the sterling bloc could be contained through direct controls.[34] Also, the British--having perhaps associated with American economists too closely for their own good--accepted the official American view that the primary problem of the United States in the postwar period would be deflation. They would adopt policies in 1946 to fit the years to come and meanwhile muddle through the transitional period.

Monitoring Exchange Controls

March 1, 1947, was the date scheduled for the Fund to begin exchange transactions and the beginning of the official transition period of five years. During the interim, exchange controls could be imposed by member countries to protect their payments positions. Except for the United States and four Central American republics, all member countries elected to impose controls. A complex system of bilateral agreements arose to control the impact of trade transactions on the non-dollar countries' reserves. A typical agreement might bind Britain and Argentina to accept specified amounts of coal and beef imports, the net peso and pound credits accumulated over a year's time to cancel out. By 1950, when the IMF made its first report on payments or restrictions, soft-currency countries (those whose currency was not freely convertible into dollars) around the world were bound together in several hundred bilateral compacts. The outlook for removal of payments restrictions by 1952, anticipated in the Agreement, was highly pessimistic.

The World Bank

The twin institution of the IMF could scarcely have held center stage during the discussions of payments problems that occupied the year-and-a-half following the Bretton Woods Conference. More concern was manifested for reserve positions than reconstruction and development. Between the two institutions, there were major differences. The Fund was presumed to have powers--to deny access to its resources, require consultation by members, declare a currency "scarce", etc. --that had no counterpart in the Bank; the Fund subscription was larger,[34] and there was an incentive--lacking in the Bank--for a country to enlarge its Fund subscription. There was the prospect, moreover, that the Fund would hum with activity from its opening day of operation, while the Bank would develop more slowly and passively.

It is clear from the Bank Agreement (Article I) that its basic role was intended to be as a guarantor of private loans, except for a brief period in which it might be required to make reconstruction loans. The subscription quota was small--$2 billion, of which only $200 million was lendable outright without member country permission--although the total capitalization was $10 billion. By borrowing on its own credit in world capital markets, however, the Bank could enlarge its lendable funds.

A primary objective of the Bank was to spread the risk of international lending over the member countries. Under the Agreement, each member country assumed a contingent liability equal to its quota for loans of the Bank. Elaborate safeguards were imposed that began with the member country guaranteeing loans to nongovernment institutions and ended with the requirement that loans be for a "specific purpose". The safeguards have drawn the criticism that they are inflexible and unreasonable.

The Bank began operations in June, 1946, and, at the time of its first annual meeting in October, 1946, it had made no loans, despite receipt of two applications. When the first loan was made in May, 1947, the Bank had been in operation nearly a year. All reconstruction loans were made in 1947--to France, Netherlands, Denmark and Luxembourg--and, contrary to the Agreement, the loans to the first three countries were "general purpose" loans for emergency assistance. Development loans were not made until 1948, and then primarily to Africa and Asia rather than Europe.

In its early years, the Bank proved of limited usefulness either for reconstruction or development. The volume of funds available was small in relation to needs, and lending rules were inflexible as regards both the letter of the Agreement and its administration. By the mid-1950's, the Bank was revising its interpretation of the Agreement and, unlike the IMF, showed considerable flexibility.

Dollar-Sterling Diplomacy

No aspect of postwar monetary developments reveals more clearly the limitations of the planning that culminated in the Bretton Woods System than American-British relations after victory had been won in Europe.

Frequent pledges by the two countries that their wartime harmony would be carried into peacetime mark the diplomatic history of the war; but the wartime harmony was frequently strained by differences in view, not least with respect to postwar monetary and financial planning. The British reaction to Article VII of the Lend-Lease Agreement, the choice of the White Plan over the Keynes Plan for Bretton Woods, and the exercise by the United States of its dominant position in the Bretton Woods Institutions have been mentioned above. Against this background the American decision to terminate Lend-Lease aid with the victory over Japan strained the American-British alliance severely.

The End of Lend-Lease

As the war in Europe drew to an increasingly predictable conclusion late in 1944, a gap in postwar financial planning became increasingly evident. Between American wartime aid and an unknown volume of private investment under the cloak of IBRD guarantees, stood only UNRRA, an organization that had been created to provide basic necessities of life in countries that had been occupied by the enemy. The failure to plan for the near-term loomed ominously to Britain because she faced serious economic threats that could be removed, if at all, only by Herculean efforts applied over several years. Chief among these threats was the necessity to revive prewar export trade that had fallen by two-thirds. Overseas investment income would be reduced because external assets had been liquidated in large volume. External liabilities, however, especially with the Sterling Area, had increased markedly. It was estimated that British exports would have to be increased by approximately 75 percent if the country were to compensate for its losses and new liabilities. Britain was enjoying wartime living levels less austere than they might have been only because Lend-Lease aid enabled her to divert resources to the civilian sector. It was logical, therefore, that she should look to Lend-Lease aid continued beyond the peace as a stop-gap to provide some of the time required to make transitional adjustments. Continuation of Lend-Lease aid during "Stage II," the period between the end of the War in Europe and the final defeat of Japan, was arranged at the Second Quebec Conference in November, 1944. But the defeat of Japan was accomplished much in advance of the expectations that underlay the Quebec Conference, and Lend-Lease Aid was terminated effective August 21, 1945, to the consternation of the British.

The British Loan

Britain's desperate financial condition left no other alternative than an American loan. For failure to prepare their respective publics with information about Britain's financial plight in the immediate postwar period, the official families in London and Washington reaped a whirlwind in the Fall of 1945. The British people, after years of waiting for the fruits of victory, were not in a suppliant mood, and some members of Parliament denied either the need for a loan or intention of requesting one. Where the need was conceded, as by Winston Churchill, Leader of the Opposition, it was framed as a payment justified by reason of Britain's greater sacrifices in the war, such as standing alone against the enemy for a year-and-a-half. In the United States the public mood was fully as much opposed to giving a loan as was the British disposition to beg for one. Despite having enjoyed an increase in living standards during the war and having been spared physical destruction, the American people and their Congress were indifferent to further involvement beyond the necessities of occupation in Europe or Asia. American subscriptions to the Bretton Woods institutions had bought peace of mind, if such were needed. Moreover, British elections had recently brought the Labor Party to power on a platform of broadscale socialization of the economy, and the American penchant for ascribing evil to all economic arrangements different from their (idealized) own asserted itself in a condescending attitude toward the British; the money would only be wasted on socialist schemes foredoomed to failure!

Keynes once again was his country's emissary to the United States, this time to encounter an obduracy in Washington that was impervious even to his persuasiveness in pleading Britain's cause. The cause, set forth in September, 1945, bore two heads: negotiation of a British Lend-Lease settlement, and a measure of aid (hopefully a grant-in-aid) amounting to $6 billion! Keynes based his appeal largely on the requirements of multilateralism; if Britain did not receive the desired aid, she would, regrettably, be forced to autarkical policies--in perpetuity. Conferences by the British and the Americans in 1963 on "Commercial Policy," the complex of tariffs and their varied application to screen imports, inevitably were drawn into these discussions. A quid pro quo was reached; Britain would accept a stern reminder of her obligations under Article VII to modify the system of Imperial Preference, make sterling freely convertible for current transactions within a year, and fund at long-term an unspecified share of the sterling balances held by British dominions. She would receive from the United States cancellation of Lend-Lease debts accrued during the war,[35] and a fifty-year loan of $3.75 billion at 2 percent interest, with interest waived during years in which inadequate foreign exchange was earned. Thus was a gap in postwar international planning closed, with an improvisation, under highly unfavorable conditions (the British hastened to close the loan and Lend-Lease settlement issues in advance of December 31, 1945, in order to ratify the Bretton Woods Agreement and be a founding member), and with an inadequate[36] loan to which were attached impossible requirements.

It is evident from Administration statements throughout 1946 that the United States persisted in the mistaken belief that--excepting the British loan to insure abandonment of Imperial Preference--Europe's financial needs during the transition would be met through private loans and the Bretton Woods institutions. During the year, however, the basic course of postwar international relations was set with the solidification of the American and Soviet blocs of countries. American economic foreign policy responded to increasing Soviet hostility by moving to control the end-use of future U.S.-supplied funds and, in 1947, by inaugurating the gigantic European Recovery Program. The policies appropriate to the United States as a large creditor would be forthcoming, but under far different motivation than originally assumed in the Bretton Woods Agreement. Multilateralism under a supranationalistic organization had been abandoned as an objective.

The withdrawal of world countries into hostile autarkies aggravated the structural dislocation produced by World War II. In general, food surpluses ended up in one bloc and finished manufactureds surpluses in another. Twenty years after the war this imbalance still threatens external equilibrium. By early 1947 all hope for early restoration of equilibrium in free world trade--kept alive during 1946 by Britain's success in sparking export trade--had been dashed. Disequilibrium, far from moderating, was deepening.

THE BRETTON WOODS SYSTEM APPRAISED

The Fund

Two categories of judgment are possible with respect to the Bretton Woods system, other than a survey of world trade and monetary relations as they developed under the system (Chapter 4). One judgment weighs the system as the culmination of original ideas, the other weighs the system as an apparatus intended to faciliate external adjustment.

The ideas that underlay the Bretton Woods System, the early drafts by White and Keynes, were bold ingenious constructs. Each man built on experience between the wars and offered a system consistent with exchange rate stability that would enable a country to adjust its external position without resort either to controls or suicidal domestic policies. Successive drafts of White's proposal reveal a step-by-step accommodation to the presumed tolerance of Congress, and perhaps the press. The "bank" concept in White's Settlement Fund was an early casualty of these revisions, as were the proposals for international currency deposits. Keynes' Plan was also pared to acceptable proportions in advance of the Bretton Woods Conference. Political realities--whatever repository of conventional wisdom is by that term implied--tempered the boldness of the system before a proposition ever was put to the Bretton Woods Conference. Was it not a mistake to settle for a shadow of the original Keynes-White concepts expecting, as did Keynes, to revise and extend the diluted product at a later time? Given the idealism of the war period, and the knowledge of how perishable war-induced idealism could be, the American and British Conferences might preferably have constructed a bold new system on the Keynes model, rather than cut the original concept to forms sufficiently mundane that they would be assured an acceptable status with the least imaginative committee chairman in the Congress.

The International Monetary Fund did not emerge from the Bretton Woods Conference as an organization through which the interwar period monetary chaos would assuredly be avoided in the future. Probably, such an assurance could not have been made even if the most ambitious plans by White or Keynes had been put into operation. Great differences in capital structure, cost levels and income--the heritage of depression and war--separated even the industrialized countries in 1947, making trade without controls very hazardous. Moreover, simultaneous with their formulation of means to maintain external equilibrium, many of the countries had formulated means to maintain internal equilibrium. These latter efforts, represented by the British Beveridge Plan and the American Employment Act, had the effect of introducing a rigidity into the adjustment process. Under the Bretton Woods System, except for the case of fundamental disequilibrium, an external deficit would be ridden out with the aid of a Fund draw. If the deficit persisted, but was not reflective of fundamental disequilibrium, limited exchange rate reductions might be made. Mechanisms of adjustment presumably included the classical wage and price adjustments. Stable rates would now have to coexist with full employment. What would provide the adjustment apparatus to restore equilibrium if exchange rates, employment levels, and (by implication) prices all were to be inflexible? Structural changes expressed through relative growth rates would be the only factor remaining to absorb the impact of adjustment, a slender reed on which to base the achievement of Bretton Woods objectives.

Despite logical faults in the adjustive mechanism provided under the Bretton Woods System, in practice equilibrating changes in prices, wages, capital flows, and, most important, U.S. aid eased postwar external adjustments. World trade expanded and internal and external equilibrium were both satisfactorily achieved, with some exceptions among the developed countries (and many less developed countries) through the decade of the 1950's.

The Bank

The World Bank's intended function was simple--to stimulate private lending through its investigator and guarantor administrative structure and elaborate procedural rules, trappings shared with its complex twin. If the fundamental article of faith underlying the Fund was that equilibrium adjustments would result if time were allowed, the related principle of the Bank was that private capital flows would mightily support equilibrating adjustments if an umbrella of guarantees were provided. In a sense, both assumptions were in varying degrees inadequate, and the failure of the U.S. and Britain to grapple with the realistic magnitude of postwar financial problems is traceable to the simple faiths on which the Bretton Woods institutions stood.

Unfinished Business

The American-British wartime discussions that mapped the requirements for postwar economic planning were oriented to six areas of interest (p.30). Of these, the quest for international organizations to provide for maintenance of exchange stability and to deal with balance of payments problems, and for similar organizati to deal with long-term international investment, and relief and reconstruction had been met before the end of 1945. An important accomplishment that the Bretton Woods conferees assumed would come into existence was an international organization for the reduction of trade barriers. Seven years of planning and negotiation culminated in the development of a code of commercial conduct that was presented to the fifty-six country Havana Conference in 1948. Fifty-four countries (including the United States) signed the Final Act of the Conference (the Charter for an International Trade Organization); but, for failure of the United States to ratify the charter, the ITO was stillborn. Provisions for negotiations to reduce trade barriers had been made in 1947 in anticipation of the establishment of ITO. In Geneva, the General Agreements on Trade and Tariffs (GATT) were concluded in 1947 and, subsequent to the ITO charter demise, renewed at Annecy in 1949, Torquay in 1950, and Geneva in 1956. A move to pick up the pieces of the ITO by formalizing GATT, and providing a more permanent machinery for trade deliberations, was entertained in 1954 by the GATT countries, and an agreement was negotiated for the creation of the Organization For Trade Cooperation. Despite the efforts of the GATT parties to tailor the agreement to American sensitivities by depriving it of any decision-making powers, the proposed organ proved too heady for the Congress and the matter was allowed to drop. Multilateralism in world trade has come to rest in regional trading associations of countries with common geography.

Postwar economic planning anticipated two other accomplishments: an international agreement on primary commodity price control, and measures to maintain full employment. With respect to commodity price control, a concern of primary producers whose fortunes are often upset by structural maladjustments attributable to the generally inelastic demand and supply functions governing their products, international agreements have been negotiated for individual commodities such as wheat. The United States has opposed efforts to establish, within the United Nations, any permanent apparatus--even a review board--to deal with commodity prices.

With respect to full employment measures, the United Nations Economic and Social Council has provided machinery for study and review of economic stabilization problems. It has become clear that inability to coordinate fiscal and monetary policies in behalf of full employment and price stability is, in the 1960's, a serious impediment to international monetary equilibrium.

The accomplishments and failures of the planning for postwar economic cooperation will concern us in succeeding chapters. Toward the end of the 1950's, however, the inherent limitations of the Bretton Woods System combined with lack of monetary and fiscal policy coordination among the major trading countries (the new economic nationalism) had created imbalances that have not, in mid-1966, proved amenable to solution.

Notes to Chapter 3

1. Bank for International Settlements, 15th Annual

Report, 1944-45, p.27.

2. Federal Reserve Bank of New York, Annual Report for 1945 (New York: Federal Reserve Bank of New York, 1946), pp.28-33.

3. The declaration was drawn up by the United States and Britain and endorsed by thirteen other countries.

4. The transformation of the Lend-Lease concept from a rationale for giving aid to countries whose aims attracted American sympathy into an instrument for securing American objectives--such as access to Commonwealth Markets on equal terms with Britain--has been detailed in numerous sources. Cordell Hull acknowledges his dismay that the Atlantic Charter did not categorically proscribe Britain's Imperial Preference Policy, and describes the methodical efforts of the Department of State to attach trade conditions to the Lend-Lease Agreement with Britain. Cordell Hull, Memoirs of Cordell Hull (New York: Macmillan, 1948), Vol. II, pp. 975-76, 1151-53, and 1476-77. Other views are Richard N. Gardner, Sterling-Dollar Diplomacy (Oxford: The Clarendon Press, 1956), pp.54-68, and W. M. Scammell, International Monetary Policy (Second Edition; London: Macmillan, 1961), pp.119-28.

5. E. F. Penrose, Economic Planning for the Peace (Princeton, N.J.: Princeton University Press, 1953), pp.39-40.

6. John Maynard Keynes, Indian Currency and Finance (London: Macmillan, 1913), and Monetary Reform (New York: Harcourt Brace, 1924).

7. R. F. Harrod, Life of John Maynard Keynes (New York: Harcourt Brace, 1951), pp.442-45.

8. Ibid. p.498.

9. Cf. Hull, op. cit., pp. 975-76, Scammell, op. cit., pp.120-21, and Gardner, op. cit., pp.54-68.

10. Harrod, op. cit., p.526.

11. Parliamentary Debates on an International Clearing

Union, House of Lords, May 18, 1943. p.76.

12. Harrod, _op. cit._, pp.526-27.

13. Joan Robinson, "The International Currency Proposals," _Economic Journal_, LIII (1943), p.161.

14. Harrod, _op. cit._, pp.528-29.

15. Gardner, _op. cit._, p.75.

16. _Ibid._, p.75.

17. _Ibid._, p.76.

18. Cf. Harrod, _op. cit._, p.515. Harrod quotes Keynes' minutes of a 1941 meeting with officials of the Treasury Department ". . . one can take nothing whatever for settled in the United States for the sufficient reason that the administration not being in control of Congress, is not in a position to enter into commitments on anything."

19. Gardner, _op. cit._, p.112.

20. In April, 1944, a document entitled "Joint Statement on the Establishment of an International Monetary Fund" was published, and this became the basis for negotiations at Bretton Woods.

21. Only half of the member countries could be borrowers at any one time and annual draws were limited to 25 percent; thus $4 billion--times--.25 equals $1 billion.

22. In years when a country's international reserves _decreased_, unless its reserves were less than its Fund quota, it was obligated to pay back half the difference between the increase in the Fund's holdings of its currency and the decrease in its reserves. (Art. V, Sec. 7, Schedule B).

23. Scammell, _op. cit._, pp.157-58.

24. Gardner, _op. cit._, pp.133-35.

25. Harrod, _op. cit._, pp.584-85.

26. Scammell, op. cit., pp.176-77.

27. Gardner, op. cit., pp.134-35.

28. Ibid., p.127.

29. Ibid., p.124.

30. Ibid., pp.125-26.

31. Ibid., p.129.

32. Lloyd A. Metzler, "Exchange Rates and the International Monetary Fund," in Lloyd A. Metzler, Robert Triffin, and Gottfried Haberler, International Monetary Policies (Washington: Board of Governors of the Federal Reserve System, 1947), pp.25-26.

33. Cf. Metzler, op. cit., pp.39-42.

34. Despite the larger IRBD capitalization, only 20 percent was subscribed, while the entire quota of the IMF was subscribed.

35. The total value of U.S. Lend-Lease claims against Britain totaled about $20 billion. Britain was held accountable for $650 million ($532 million for Lend-Lease supplies in her possession at the end of the war in Europe plus $118 million in the "pipeline"); thus $19.4 billion was cancelled.

36. The total from the U.S. and Canada approximated $5 billion.

CHAPTER 4 EMERGENCE OF A U.S. BALANCE OF PAYMENTS PROBLEM

STRUGGLE FOR CONVERTIBILITY, 1947-58

One of the studies of post-World War II international monetary relations declares 1947 to have marked 'the end of Bretton Woods.'[1] If the expectation was that the Bretton Woods institutions would be able, unaided, to cope with balance of payments crises regardless of their scope and magnitude, the judgment may be deserved. But the IMF and IBRD were not fitted out even to bear the burdens of a smooth transition between wartime and peacetime world monetary relations, and the transition turned out to be crisis-ridden, rather than smooth. Effective means of dealing with Europe's transitional needs were devised after the United States was shocked into a realization of Europe's actual need for aid by the events of 1947, and it is idle to lament that the means were national (U.S. aid) rather than international and motivated in part by political aims (to counter the Communist threat in Europe) rather than a pure passion for multilateral trade or imaginative creditorship. A decade later than the Bretton Woods participants had expected, interconvertibility of currencies was an accomplished fact and the dollar shortage was over. The GATT apparatus remained a limping substitute for ITO, and the White House, within a few years, contained a Special Representative for Trade Negotiations, signifying a change of heart on previous attitudes toward ITO and OTC. Bilateralism, after 1958, was of historical interest only. In its place regional trade and payments unions had arisen (with U.S. support) posing wholly new problems for multilateralism in world trade, and the United States was challenged to develop a strategy to preserve the strength of the dollar and the pound against pressures unforeseen until they were revealed in the end-of-decade balance of payments statistics.

From the End of the War to the Marshall Plan

World War II induced extremely large changes in the balance of payments accounts of the United States.

From a net receipts position on current and long-term capital transactions that averaged nearly $1 billion during the years 1936-40, the accounts moved to a net payments position averaging more than $1 billion during the years 1941-45. Table 2 shows these data. The change in position was produced by profound shifts in government unilateral transfers and long-term capital; in 1942 these two magnitudes totaled $6.4 billion, in 1943, $12.5 billion, in 1944, $14.0 billion, and in 1945, $7.5 billion. During the five-year period, 1936-40, the comparable amount of these payments averaged $40 million. It is in the context of these extraordinary net payments that the transition problems faced by the recipients of U.S. wartime aid must be viewed. The abrupt termination of Lend-Lease aid, for example, because of the earlier-than-expected conclusion of the war against Japan, caused disturbances for which no adequate compensation had been planned at Bretton Woods.

In 1946 a shift in U.S. external accounts of more than $2 billion occurred, compared with the average 1941-45 net payments (from net payments of $1.2 billion to net receipts of $1.1 billion). Compared to 1945, the 1946 U.S. balance represented an increase of $3.7 billion net receipts. This magnitude was exceeded by the U.S. balance in 1947 of $3.4 billion in net receipts an increase of $2.3 billion compared to 1946, and $4.6 billion compared to 1941-45 average. Western Europe found itself with a net payments deficit vis-à-vis the United States of more than $1 billion in 1946 and, despite substantial loans to Britain, France, and Italy, nearly $.5 billion in 1947. U.S. gold purchases from Western Europe in the first two postwar years amounted to nearly $1.5 billion. The road to convertibility (removal of exchange controls and other impediments that restricted residents' and nonresidents' freedom to transfer their claims to accounts outside a given country) was being made very difficult because the chief candidates for an early attempt at convertibility were being denuded of their reserve assets.

The grim world monetary outlook reflected disappointment of the hopes for continuation of wartime alliances in a smooth transition to peacetime trade relationships. From the spring of 1946 on, however, the countries of the world began to orient themselves increasingly to either

TABLE 2

INTERNATIONAL TRANSACTIONS OF THE UNITED STATES, 1936-52
(Millions of Dollars)

Period	Excess Receipts (+) Or Payments (-)			Net Inflow (+) Or Outflow (-) of Funds On Gold And Short-term Capital Account				Errors and Omissions
	Net, Current and Long-term Capital Transactions	Net, Goods and Services and Unilateral Transfers	Net, Long-term Capital[1]	Net, Total	Changes in U.S. Official Reserve Assets [Increase (-)]	Net Movement of		
						U. S. Short-term Capital	Foreign Short-term Capital	
Average, 1948-52	-1,229	+ 8	-1,237	+ 610	- 138	- 35	+ 783	+ 619
1948	- 236	+1,915	-2,151	- 957	-1,736	-110	+ 885	+1,193
1947	+3,444	+8,904	-5,460	-4,393	-3,315	-189	- 889	+ 949
1946	+1,084	+4,822	-3,738	-1,302	- 623	-310	- 369	+ 218
1945	-2,649	-1,072	-1,577	+2,641	+ 548	- 96	+2,189	+ 8
1944	-1,737	-1,690	- 47	+1,774	+1,350	- 85	+ 509	- 37
Average, 1941-45	-1,176	- 656	- 520	+1,082	+ 392	- 15	+ 705	+ 94
Average, 1936-40	+ 961	+ 695	+ 266	-1,540	-2,370	+107	+ 723	+ 579

Sources: For Years 1936-45, Balance of Payments Statistical Supplement, (Revised Edition; Washington, D. C.: 1963) pp.1-3; for years 1946-65, Survey of Current Business, June, 1966, pp.24-25.

[1]Excludes undistributed profits of subsidiaries.

the U.S. or Soviet "blocs," and the illusion of continuing U.S.-Soviet amity vanished. For fifteen years thereafter the IMF marked time, while the world moved away from the principles of Bretton Woods then painfully began to work its way back toward them. Meanwhile, to protect their scarce exchange reserves from erosion, many countries resorted to bilateral agreements and direct control over foreign exchange--the antithesis of Bretton Woods. Even these desperate moves afforded only precarious equilibrium at levels of consumption and investment significantly below prewar standards. By early 1947 Europe's economic plight had become a threat to its political stability; strong bids for political control were being made by Communist parties in Italy, France, and Greece. In response to this crisis the United States developed a program of long-term assistance profoundly different from its previously declared policy. Henceforth, U.S. aid would be unilateral and tied to American foreign policy rather than extended through international organizations with disregard for political values.

The United States, recognizing the division between two blocs--Soviet Union-Eastern Europe and the United States-Western Europe--as a fait accompli, used its influence on the Boards of Governors of the IMF and IBRD to insulate these institutions from the Soviet Bloc. Since the Soviet Union had not ratified the Bretton Woods Agreement, the effect of this move was felt primarily by the Soviet satellite countries that were members. In mid-1947 the IBRD declared that it did not consider its nonpolitical character to mean that it was obliged to ignore political events in making loans, explaining "....there is an obvious and necessary interrelation and interaction between political events and conditions in any country. The soundness of a loan depends fundamentally on the financial and economic prospects of the borrower. Insofar as those prospects may be affected by the conditions of political instability or uncertainty in the borrowing country, those political conditions must be taken into consideration."[2] This interpretation was the basis for the Bank refusing to lend Poland funds later in the year. The Fund also asserted its intention to consider the economic and financial factors that might prejudice the use of its lending powers in strict conformity to the Articles of

Agreement.[3] Strict interpretation of the Bank and Fund Articles created hardships for members not affiliated with the Soviet Bloc because it resulted in a virtual moratorium on Bank and Fund activities.

The Marshall Plan

Western Europe's difficult economic problems of 1946 were transformed into a state of desperation by the severe winter of 1946-47. Traditional sources of food products were either slow to reach prewar production levels or were, as exemplified by East Germany and Poland, absorbed into the Soviet Bloc and unavailable to Western Europe. Shortages of dollar exchange hampered Western European imports from the United States. The dollar scarcity problem was made worse by the terms of trade; raw material import prices tended to be high and finished manufactured export prices low. Private capital from abroad was repelled by the spectre of economic and political instability and failed to play its expected role in reconstruction. The immediate, desperate need was dollar exchange or credits to support imports from the United States.

The first move by the United States toward reconstruction of the world's dollar receipts position to levels nearer those of the 1941-45 period was precipitated indirectly by the deteriorating British balance of payments. Britain was forced to reduce her overseas military commitments because of her import needs and informed the United States that British forces aiding the Greek government in its struggle with Communist insurgents would have to be withdrawn. Greece and Turkey, alone among the countries of Southeastern Europe had withstood absorption into the Soviet Bloc, and the response of the United States was immediate. An appropriation of $400 million was voted by the Congress for economic and military assistance to the two countries. The catalyst that precipitated a similar response to Western Europe's dollar scarcity problem--the first cause of the Greek-Turkish aid program--was continuing evidence of Soviet hostility. Peace treaty negotiations were hamstrung by Soviet intransigency and the call went out in mid-1947 for a meeting of world Communist Party leaders in Warsaw, including those from Western Europe. The meeting effectively reconstituted the infamous Third International[4], the vehicle of world revolution that had been disbanded by the Soviet Union in 1944 during the "United Front" period of international Communism. In this atmosphere the Congress found itself able to accept several bitter pills--the complete breakdown of the 1946 British Loan Agreement provisions,[5] provision of Greek-Turkish Aid, and the necessity to rise to Secretary Marshall's impassioned plea for a coherent program of long-term aid to facilitate European economic recovery. The Secretary warned, "The truth of the matter is that Europe's requirements for the next three years for foreign food and other essential products--principally from America--are so much greater than her present ability to pay that she must have substantial additional help, or face economic, social, and political deterioration..."[6]

The Economic Cooperation Act[7] was passed in April, 1948. It provided for a four-year European Recovery Program to be completed with American assistance. Self-help and mutual aid were expected of Europe, and "bilateral and multilateral undertakings, a joint organization, and the acceptance of collective responsibility for recommending allocation of United States aid"[8] were required. The assistance provided was to be in the form of "tied grants," but with sufficient flexibility to shift purchases of products in short supply to foreign sources, and to attract to the United States purchases of products (particularly agricultural products) in surplus supply. It was tacitly assumed that the recovery of Europe "was a prerequisite for achieving the general aims of United States commercial and financial policy," and "that in the interests of American security strong measures had to be taken to check the advance of Communism in Europe."[9] West Germany, previously an occupied enemy territory, was to be included in the European Recovery Program.

The passage of ERP legislation indicated profound changes in the foreign economic policy assumptions that the U.S. had held at the end of World War II. Hopes for cooperation with the Soviet Union had turned to fears of Soviet expansion. The temptation to consign Germany and Japan to perpetual lesser-power status had become infeasible because of the Communist menace to Europe and Asia. Illusions that Europe would quickly recover prewar levels of production and move deliberately to install multilateralism as the dominant basis of world trade had been drastically revised. The United States was willing to require regional bilateral and multilateral trade arrangements in order to accomplish Europe's recovery and hold in abeyance attempts to achieve the much-desired goal of multilateralism.

European Monetary Cooperation. In anticipation of ERP, European countries undertook the formation of organizations to settle intra-European payments imbalances more efficiently. The Committee of European Economic Cooperation,[10] meeting in Paris during 1947, developed a clearing pool arrangement that would reduce the volume of debtor country foreign payments requiring gold or dollar settlement. The first agreement on multilateral monetary compensation[11] established by CEEC reluctantly adopted a more conventional system for mutual offsetting of claims and debts by parties to bilateral agreements.[12] Under the system, country A would settle its indebtedness to country B by abandoning its claim on country C, and so forth, so long as the chain continued. The small volume of debts settled by this arrangement indicates its lack of success, although similar arrangements operated for nearly three years and served as a point of departure from the bilateral agreements that had strangled European trade in 1946 and 1947.

When ERP aid began operation in the spring of 1948, allocations to particular countries were based in part on their prospective dollar and other "hard currency" deficits. Grants were labeled "direct" or "conditional," and the conditional grants required recipient countries to grant drawing rights to countries whose balances with them might be in deficit position as determined from monthly forecasts. This system of bilateral settlements enjoyed limited success. It has been criticized by Triffin, who argues that the stimulus to European trade attributable to pre-1950 monetary arrangements was slight compared to ERP aid.[13]

In September, 1950, an ingenious international clearing system was formed among the OEEC countries. This system, the European Payments Union, countered the existing bilateral arrangements that had frustrated European trade and paved the way for full convertibility of European currencies. The principle of EPU was a settlement fund which became a party to clearing transactions among OEEC countries involving balances in intra-European trade. U.S. contributions and individual country quotas created the fund. Bilateral balances were transferred into debtor-creditor balances with EPU and, following initial satisfaction of their creditors, countries made payments to EPU (and received credits) in varying proportions of (1) gold and/or dollars and (2) EPU credit. The proportion of gold or dollars to EPU credit in any particular settlement depended upon the cumulative debtor or creditor position of a country with the Union,[14] and the proportion was graduated so as to induce debtors to clear their balances. A country's drawing rights in the Union were automatic up to the limit of its quota. Because the dollar-shortage of OEEC countries was a general problem, and the countries traded chiefly with each other, the EPU was a highly successful interim arrangement to encourage trade and prepare Europe for a multilateral exchange system. When convertibility of European currencies was ultimately achieved in 1958, the raison d'être of EPU vanished and it was succeeded by the European Monetary Agreement under an arrangement agreed upon in advance.

The End of Dollar Scarcity. The dollar payment requirements of the countries outside the Soviet Bloc exceeded normal receipts and reserves by an estimated $6.8 billion in 1946, $9.7 billion in 1947, and $5.1 billion in 1948.[15] The magnitude of these deficits despite imposition of stringent controls precipitated financial crises in Europe. However, the dollar deficit declined as a result of large U.S. grants and loans until it was virtually eliminated in 1950. This dramatic improvement was a temporary effect of U.S. military procurement for the Korean War, and the years 1951 and 1952 brought resumption of dollar deficits estimated at $3.2 and $1.4 billion.[16]

In the period of greatest dollar scarcity the IMF did not declare the dollar scarce under Article VII of the IMF Articles. The Fund hoarded its dollars and dollars thus failed to become "scarce" under the Article's definitions.

Table 2 shows the detail of the U.S. balance on current and capital transactions in the postwar years and comparative balances for the prewar and postwar years.

In 1948 the U.S. ran a net payments position of $236 million, a swing of $1.3 billion from the 1946 net receipts position and $3.7 billion from the 1947 position. For the five years, 1948-52, the U.S. net payments position averaged $1.2 billion, the direct result of government grants and loans that averaged nearly $4 billion annually. U.S. private long-term capital payments during this period averaged less than $1 billion, and obviously could not have been relied upon to cushion the world dollar deficit in the absence of government programs; early postwar planning had, however, placed primary reliance on private capital to meet reconstruction needs. As U.S. private long-term capital exports increased in the years after 1952, performing their equilibrating role, government grants declined. Table 3 shows the shifting mix of U.S. government and private payments that helped finance the dollar deficit during the postwar period.

TABLE 3

FINANCING OF THE DOLLAR DEFICIT
(Billions of Dollars)

Period	Total Grants and Loans	U.S. Government Grants *	U.S. Government Loans	Private Long-Term Loans
1946	5.5	2.3	3.0	.2
1947	6.9	1.9	4.2	.8
1948	5.7	3.9	1.0	.8
1949	6.1	5.0	.7	.4
1950	3.8	3.5	.2	.1
1951	4.1	3.0	.2	.9
1952	3.5	2.0	.4	1.1
1953	2.3	1.9	.2	.2
1954	2.9	1.6	.1	1.2
1955	3.3	1.9	.3	1.1
1956	4.9	1.7	.6	2.6
1957	5.9	1.6	1.0	3.3

Source: Survey of Current Business, June, 1966, pp.24-25.

* Excludes military grants.

Table 4 summarizes the U.S. net balance on current and long-term capital transactions during various periods from 1948 to 1965.[17] The average net payments position during the periods 1948-52 and 1953-57 was approximately the same. Toward the end of the 1953-57 period (1956) private capital exports (net) passed the $2 billion dollar annual level, and the 1958, 1959, 1960, and 1960-65 data reflect sharply increased levels of private capital exports, as the U.S. net receipts position declined to slightly more than half the 1948-57 level. U.S. gold and reserve assets stocks and short-term capital shifted to a net outflow basis after 1957. By 1958 the problem of dollar scarcity had ended. In the years ahead the dollar would weaken on the world exchanges as a consequence of oversupply, a turn of events unimagined a few years earlier.[18]

Convertibility[19] Achieved

Britain's unfortunate experience with convertibility in 1947, an exercise she entered upon reluctantly at the insistence of the United States, was sufficient proof to other countries of the hazards that lay in the wake of a premature free-exchange policy. The lesson influenced the course of events with respect to convertibility. When the CEEC had tried to promote a European clearing system in 1947, it drew insufficient support because of fears that scarce exchange reserves would vanish, and ultimately Europe settled for the modest First Agreement on Multilateral Compensation. European convertibility hinged in large part upon the strength of the pound sterling as a reserve currency and, therefore, upon Britain's balance of payments position.

The years 1947-51 were for Britain the critical postwar years. Following the abortive convertibility attempt in 1947, Britain suffered successively from adverse terms of trade (import prices increased nearly 20 percent during 1947), inflation, an American recession, and speculation against the overvalued pound. In the first nine months of 1949, Britain lost nearly one-third of her gold and dollar reserves, and before the end of the year was forced to devalue the pound by 30 percent.[20] A large number of countries followed Britain's move within a few days, including France for the second time in successive years.[21] Korean war procurement by the United States after June, 1950, was

TABLE 4

INTERNATIONAL TRANSACTIONS OF THE UNITED STATES, 1948-65
(Millions of Dollars)

Period	Excess Receipts (+) Or Payments (-)			Net Inflow (+) Or Outflow (-) of Funds On Gold And Short-term Capital Account				Errors and Omissions
	Net, Current and Long-term Capital Transactions	Net, Goods and Services and Unilateral Transfers	Net, Long-term Capital[1]	Net, Total	Changes in U.S. Official Reserve Assets [Increase (-)][2]	Net Movement of: U. S. Short-term Capital	Net Movement of: Foreign Short-term Capital	
Average, 1960-65	- 772	+3,362	-4,134	+1,588	+1,009	- 936	+1,515	-816
1960	-1,375	+1,684	-3,059	+2,316	+2,143	-1,348	+1,521	-941
1959	-3,542	-2,301	-1,241	+3,119	+1,035	- 97	+2,161	+423
1958	-3,541	- 155	-3,386	+3,030	+2,292	- 311	+1,049	+511
Average, 1953-57	-1,301	+ 378	-1,680	+ 736	- 24	- 290	+1,049	+565
Average, 1948-52	-1,229	+ 8	-1,237	+ 610	- 138	- 35	+ 783	+619

Source: Survey of Current Business, June, 1966, pp.24-25.

[1]Excludes undistributed profits of subsidiaries.

[2]Reflects $259 million payment of gold portion of U.S. subscription to the International Monetary Fund in 1965.

accompanied by rapid increases in world raw material prices that adversely affected Britain's payments position but benefited the overseas Sterling Area countries. When, in the following year, the overseas sterling countries suffered decreases in income as a result of price decreases, another sterling crisis threatened; but Britain resorted to internal and external controls and withstood the crisis. By early 1954 the pound, having survived three sterling crises, enjoyed a substantial degree of de facto convertibility; but sterling crises occurred in 1955, 1956, and 1957.

In Continental Europe the path to convertibility was obstructed by the great differences among countries with respect to wartime physical destruction (the Netherlands suffered the least physical damage to production facilities; France suffered the greatest damage), inflation (Germany, Belgium, and the Netherlands had relatively little inflation, France and Italy serious inflation), and adverse developments in the terms of trade. The patient adaptation of the OEEC countries to the necessity for monetary cooperation that culminated in the European Payments Union was an important factor in the eventual restoration of a powerful regional economic bloc. American aid worked with greater leverage on European problems because fewer dollars were required to settle intra-European deficits. Wide swings in surplus and deficit positions were permitted to work themselves out within a setting similar to the original Keynes Plan for the Bretton Woods conference.[22] At one time or another each of the major European trading countries faced a payments crisis under EPU. The trend, none the less, was toward liberalization of trade and currency controls, at first within the Union and gradually on an extra-Union scope.

By mid-1955 the EPU member countries felt a sufficient degree of confidence in their currencies that they specified in their renewal agreement procedures for terminating the Union and shifting responsibility for monetary cooperation to a "European IMF" provided for under the European Monetary Agreement. This agreement specified the payments practices to be followed in the post-EPU period. As a spur to promote convertibility, the members agreed to an increase in the proportion of gold and dollars required in settlement of EPU balances.

At the end of 1958, with the pound and mark (and some other currencies) already enjoying de facto convertibility, appropriate notifications[23] were made by Belgium-Luxembourg, France, Germany, Italy, the Netherlands, and Britain that they wished their currencies to be convertible outside the Union. A smooth transfer followed in which short-term credits were provided by the European Fund (created by the European Monetary Agreement) rather than EPU. Settlements in dollars at an exchange rate known in advance were guaranteed to each member's central bank for its holdings in other members' currencies through the Multilateral System of Settlements. Scammell, who scorns the procedures of the IMF, including its transitional arrangements[24], offers a different judgment of the OEEC's carefully considered transitional arrangements.[25]

> A certain ingenuity and spirit of compromise went into the making of these arrangements. They were flexible yet they provided for most of the foreseeable contingencies. While they simplified the mechanism of EPU they maintained its framework in the clearing mechanism in order to allow an orderly retreat from convertibility should that be necessary. On the other hand, if as time passed, the new system became progressively durable, this clearing system might well wither away as the bulk of settlements came to be made in the ordinary foreign exchange market.

The cautious approach of the OEEC countries to convertibility is indicated by the period that elapsed between incorporation of the European Monetary Agreement in the EPU renewal agreement (June, 1955) and its implementation with the termination of EPU (December, 1958). Once established, EMA experienced infrequent use of its Fund and Settlements System--an indication of how firmly the foundation for convertibility had been prepared and how sound the currencies of the constituent countries had become.

<u>World Monetary Reserves Restored</u>

The strength of European currencies that enabled OEEC countries to terminate the EPU in 1958 was directly related to the rapidly increasing gold and dollar reserves of their central banks. In 1958 alone, gold and dollar assets of Western Europe increased $2.9 billion ($2.3 gold, $.6 billion dollars). Britain accounted for $.5 billion (-$.9 gold, $1.4 dollars) of this total and Continental Western Europe $2.4 billion ($1.4 gold, $1.0 dollars). U.S. short-term liabilities to Europe increased from $2.5 billion in 1948 to $7.5 billion in 1958. Total U.S. short-term liabilities to foreigners increased from $7.7 billion in 1948 to $16.2 billion in 1958. World gold reserves (excluding the U.S. increased from $6.8 billion in 1948 to $17.5 billion in 1958, largely as a result of U.S. gold losses.

After 1958--the year that marks the end of the post-war dollar scarcity period--world monetary problems assumed a different hue. European central banks, which traditionally hold a large proportion of their monetary reserves in the form of gold, refused to accumulate dollars earned in trade with the U.S. in unlimited amount and began to convert a share of each year's earnings into gold. The U.S. monetary problem in international trade had come full circle; for ten years U.S. policies had supplied dollars to a world in which dollars were scarce, but henceforth, U.S. policies would have to adjust to the reality of dollar redundancy. Official settlements of dollar imbalances had assumed a new significance in U.S. external accounts.

THE DEFICIT BECOMES A BURDEN

The turnabout in the international position of the dollar was a more shocking discovery to the American people than the realization ten years before that Americ aid would be required in massive amounts to secure an independent Europe. No effort had been made to prepare the American people for either event. Reference has already been made to the widely held conviction that the dollar scarcity problem was a permanent fixture of international finance, a conviction that tended to linger after the facts no longer supported it. The Suez crisis of 1956-57, which produced a temporary net receip position in the U.S. balance of payments, masked the pro lem inherent in U.S. external disequilibrium. Non-convertibility of European currencies with respect to no resident accounts prior to 1958 also tended to obscure the growing strength of those currencies and the weakeni of the dollar. Convertibility, when it was finally declared (practically in 1958, de jura in 1961), precipitated no substantial liquidation of European currencies for conversion into dollars; European reserves, being large, obviated the necessity for any "test" of strength, and the dollar had become less attractive. Indeed, the Treaty of Rome (1958) inaugurating the European Economic Community (the "Common Market") excited U.S. commercial interest in the Common Market and attracted a steadily rising volume of U.S. private investment funds. Investment of U.S. private capital reached levels after 1962 that induced U.S. Government policies to restrict its outflow.

European Recovery and the Dollar

The desire of the United States to restore and enlarge European markets for American goods and services had figured in U.S. foreign economic policy from 1941 and Article VII of the Lend-Lease Agreement. Accordingly, the rapid pace of European economic recovery and growth, in which ERP funds were a helpful but not decisive factor, was welcomed in the United States. By the end of 1948 the prewar (1938) Gross National Product (constant prices) of the OEEC countries had been surpassed, and by 1952 it was 23 percent above prewar levels.[26] Economic growth in the Common Market averaged 5.6 percent per year 1950-60,[27] and by 1965 constant dollar GNP was approximately double the prewar level. Western Europe had fulfilled the objectives of American aid by the late 1950's, was unified, economically strong, and an ally within the North Atlantic Treaty Organization.

Economic Integration

Proposals for unification of Europe in modern times date from post-World War I and have a complex lineage.[28] The United States was hostile to all ideas of European economic integration in the years before the World War II, seeing in them a threat to U.S. economic interests.[29] During World War II no official consideration was given to unification (despite frequent reference to the idea in Prime Minister Churchill's speeches), in part because of fear that American-Soviet relations would be adversely affected.[30] In the immediate postwar period extensive discussion of the unification issue took place in the U.S. State Department and a series of internal memoranda prepared by Department committees emphasized the desirability of European political unification as a strategic counter-Soviet move, and the necessity for economic coordination to achieve European recovery.[31] By mid-1949, according to Beloff, "...the majority view in the United States already looked toward some kind of Western European political union under a general Atlantic guarantee."[32] American support for European unification was promoted by the American Committee on United Europe (formed by Allen Dulles and Senators Fulbright and George, but eventually involving about one hundred distinguished businessmen and members of Congress), which sponsored lecture tours by prominent European "integrationists," such as Winston Churchill, Jean Monet, and others, and generally propagandized in favor of European union.[33]

U.S. policy throughout the 1950's was officially one of encouragement to plans for economic and political unification but noninvolvement in any Atlantic Community, which was interpreted to mean some degree of North American-Western European integration. The signing of treaties in turn for the North Atlantic Treaty Organization, the European Coal and Steel Community (1951), the European Defense Community (1952),[34] the European Economic Community ("Common Market") and European Atomic Energy Community (EURATOM), both in 1957, and the European Free Trade Association (1959), together with increasing strength in the OEEC countries' balances of payments, brought a change in the U.S. policy of noninvolvement in an Atlantic Community. The Treaty of Rome, among Continental Western European countries, especially stirred U.S. apprehensions over the consequences of U.S. noninvolvement. In 1960, the Organization for Economic Cooperation and Development, a reorganization of the OEEC to include the United States, Canada, and Japan, was negotiated commencing a new period in U.S. policy toward European economic and political integration.

The Impact of the Common Market on U.S. Trade

The absence of Britain from the Common Market was the result of long-standing British policy, continued in the postwar period, that viewed British trading interests in terms of the Sterling Area with a close political orientation to the United States rather than Continental Europe. Britain rejected involvement with the Coal and Steel Community when it was formed in 1951, and the nationalist track taken by France beginning in 1958 under de Gaulle did nothing to increase British interest in Common Market participation. When Britain expressed a change of heart about Common Market membership in mid-1961, encouraged in some degree by contrasting U.S. attitudes of coolness toward the Free Trade Association and warm solicitude for the Common Market, her entry was blocked by de Gaulle policies based firmly on _la grandeur de la France_ and vitiation of remembered Anglo-American slights in years gone by. American foreign economic policy, which had been concerned for nearly twenty years with achievement of an open commercial policy for the Sterling Area, now faced, with Britain, the threat of possible extra-Common Market commercial policies injurious to American and British exports. Henceforth the United States and Britain, the "key currency" countries, would strive to achieve external equilibrium under singularly disadvantageous conditions while the Common Market countries accumulated claims against them.

American commercial policy, after supporting the General Agreements on Tariffs and Trade (GATT) beginning in 1947, remained largely stalemated during the 1950's chiefly due to protectionist influences on the Congress. The exclusions permitted the United States under GATT, especially the "peril point" provisions, although minor exceptions to a generally free-trade policy, were highly publicized and created the illusion abroad of American hypocrisy. In this atmosphere the threat inherent in the Common Market was its political and economic power;[35] the United States would have to adapt its commercial policies to the reality that the six member countries could now retaliate in concert against resolutions of tariff and trade questions in which the primary regard was for difficulties experienced by domestic industries.[36] With a suggestion of virtue being made of necessity, the United States passed the Trade Expansion Act in response to President Kennedy's special message to Congress, January, 1962. Authority had been sought by the President to engage in tariff bargaining primarily for the purpose of securing reductions in the general tariffs of the Common Market. At length, the Office of Special Representative for Trade Negotiations was established in the Executive branch.

The Deficit Becomes a Burden

In summary, the organization of the Common Market threatened significant changes in the historical trade relationships between the United States and the six constituent countries of continental Western Europe. This result followed not primarily from any change in the trading capability of the six countries, but from the political and economic power conferred by their unity. A common trade-policy could now be determined by the members and backed up by their concerted market power as the largest trading unit in the world economy. The emergence of a stubborn balance of payments disequilibrium concurrent with the formation of the Common Market, if it did not account for the existence of the disequilibrium, at least made the restoration of equilibrium more difficult by restricting the range of U.S. policy choices. It is in this sense that the U.S. overall balance of payments position became a burden.

MEASURING THE DEFICIT

Tables 2, 3 and 4, above, traced the net balance of the United States on goods and services, unilateral transfers (excluding military grants), and long-term capital during the pre-World War II, war, and postwar periods. The "balance" shown in the tables has a limited usefulness--to show shifts in the U.S. balance on one of many possible selections of so-called basic transactions over time. But the status of the dollar, as both a key currency and a reserve currency calls for a different measure of the total U.S. balance on external account, a measure that reveals the change in total claims against the dollar held by foreigners and the gold and reserve currencies available to meet them. The concept of payments balance employed by the Department of Commerce from the mid-1950's until June, 1966, to measure changes in the U.S. balance on a liquidity basis is described by the Department's Balance of Payments Division head, Walther Lederer, as follows:[37]

> The analysis (of the balance of payments) which I believe to be more useful (than any alternative) is designed to meet essentially a practical purpose: To measure the changes in our capability to defend the exchange value of the dollar. This defense is the responsi-

> bility of our monetary authorities and their capability depends upon their liquid resources and the claims which can be exercised against these resources.

Implicit in the liquidity measure of the over-all balance is the assumption, justified during the years before convertibility of world currencies was restored, but unjustified afterward, that all foreign dollar claims--private as well as official--could be acquired by foreign monetary authorities and converted into gold. An asymmetry in the liquidity concept exists because the claims of U.S. bank and nonbank institutions against foreigners are treated as capital outflows on the questionable ground that they could not be used (because of absence of capital controls in the United States) to defend the dollar. Thus, by the Department of Commerce liquidity balance a repatriation of U.S. short-term private capital from abroad "improves" the over-all balance, while an inflow of foreign short-term private capital (because it is viewed as a means of settling the "above-the-line" transactions) does not. Generally speaking, the liquidity concept of over-all balance exaggerates the degree of disequilibrium the U.S. is experiencing in its external position.

Dissatisfaction with the balance of payments statistics and the prevailing concept of over-all balance became rife[38] as the U.S. deficits approached the $4 billion mark (on the liquidity basis) in 1959 and 1960. A review committee of university, IMF, and business economists was appointed by the Bureau of the Budget in 1963 to study the conceptual difficulties of balance of payments accounting and problems relating to the collection, presentation, and analysis of data. The review and recommendations of the committee, known as the Bernstein Committee, were published in 1965,[39] and the Department of Commerce, responding to the committee's recommendations, revised its balance of payments data and published in the June, 1966, Survey of Current Business an additional concept of over-all balance for years 1960 and after, the balance on official reserve transactions.

The Bernstein Committee Review

The committee report makes an instructive declaration in its review of measures depicting the over-all U.S. payments balance.[40]

> The definition and measurement of a balance of payments surplus or deficit is a matter of analysis rather than accounting. Particularly complex problems arise in the case of the United States because it is a reserve currency country and banking center. No single number can adequately describe the international payments position of this country at any time.

The committee acknowledged the "legitimate need" for summary indicators of the U.S. external position, however, but criticized the Department of Commerce international liquidity concept as "unsatisfactory in principle and difficult to apply in practice."[41] No disagreement was registered by the committee with respect to the objective that the liquidity measure was intended to serve--the ability of the United States monetary authorities to defend the dollar internationally--but the liquidity concept was too broad, in some respects, and too narrow in others, to reveal the dollar's exposure. In recommending an alternative measure of balance--the balance on official reserve transactions--the committee described the context in which the defense of the dollar is undertaken.[42]

> In the present international financial system, the key demarcation in international transactions is between those of the monetary authorities and all other transactions. Leading countries have established fixed parities for their currencies and have undertaken by international agreement to maintain exchange rates within prescribed margins (one percent) of those parities. The monetary authorities use reserves to prevent a decline below this limit and acquire reserves to prevent a rise above this limit in the foreign exchange value of their currencies. In effect, the monetary authorities fill the gap between private demand for and the private supply of foreign exchange, and the size of this gap, measured by the transactions of the monetary authorities,

> provides the most useful starting point for balance of payments analysis.

The committee, in recommending the official settlements concept of over-all balance comprising official reserve transactions and prepayment of official debts to the United States, stressed the lesser problems of measurement it posed as compared with the prevailing liquidity concept and then cited two additional advantages for its choice:[43]

> First, it can be made internationally symmetrical, so that, after taking account of net additions to the world's gold reserves, surpluses would equal deficits if the same definitions were used by all countries. Second, the official settlements concept provides a measure of the surplus or deficit that is less subject to errors and omissions, as U.S. data on liabilities to foreign monetary authorities are more reliable than those on liabilities to other foreigners.

One advantage of the official settlements balance that appealed to those who desired to increase public understanding of the U.S. deficit was that, in a period of equilibrium, the deficit would be zero. Bernstein[44] and others have argued that U.S. balance of payments equilibrium, under measures based on the international liquidity concept, is achieved with an average deficit over several years of from $500 to $800 million.

The Balance Measured by Alternative Concepts

Table 5 presents data for years 1960-66 showing the U.S. over-all balance on "basic" transactions (A), the Department of Commerce Balance of Payments Division international liquidity basis (B), and the balance on official reserve transactions basis (C). The implications of the balance struck on any particular basis, which depends solely on the transactions that are included or excluded, require separate explanation of each basis.

The Basic Balance Basis. This concept of the balance rests on the assumption that transactions can be classified either as "autonomous" or "accommodating" (also

TABLE 5

U.S. BALANCE OF INTERNATIONAL PAYMENTS, 1958-66

(Millions of Dollars)[1]

	1958	1959	1960	1961	1962	1963	1964	1965	1966[7]	References, SCB, June, 1966: Table	Page	Line(s)
1. Balance on goods and services[1]	2206	147	4046	5621	5130	5897	8490	6957	----	1	25	24
2. U.S. Gov't grants and capital[2]	-3332	-2801	-3467	-3512	-3770	-4448	-4439	-4369	----	"	"	26+41
3. Private long-term capital, U.S. and foreign[3]	-2545	-1574	-2081	-2092	-1745	-2959	-3805	-4403	----	"	"	32-(38+40)-[50-(55+58+59)]
A. Balance on basic transactions basis (1+2+3)	-3671	-4228	-1502	17	-385	-1510	246	-1815	----	----	----	----
4. U.S. private short-term capital	-311	-77	-1348	-1556	-544	-785	-2146	761	----	"	"	38+40
5. Foreign commercial credits	106	12	-90	175	-115	-23	113	146	----	"	"	55
6. Errors and omissions	511	423	-941	-1006	-1159	-352	-1011	-429	----	"	"	60
B. Balance on BPD[4] liquidity basis (A+4+5+6)	-3365	-3870	-3881	-2370	-2203	-2670	-2798	-1337	-1322	3	30	3
7. Foreign private short-term capital other than commercial credits	----	----	289	1083	213	619	1554	132	----	7	35	1-2
8. Foreign holdings of U.S. Gov't bonds and notes, except official monetary institutions[5]	----	----	----	----	254	-16	154	138	----	3	30	20
9. Foreign official short-term capital, except official monetary institutions[5]	----	----	----	----	----	9	148	-38	----	"	"	19
C. Balance on official reserve transactions basis[6] (B+7+8+9)	----	----	-3402	-1347	-2706	-2044	-1546	-1305	-848	"	"	13

Source: *Survey of Current Business*, June, 1966. Table 1, pp.24-25, and Department of Commerce news release, August 17, 1966, U.S. Balance of Payments in Second Quarter 1966. Compilation based on *Report of the Review Committee for Balance of Payments Statistics*, April, 1965, Table 9.1, p.104.

1. Excludes transfers under military grants.
2. Includes private remittances and government pensions.
3. Excludes foreign holdings of U.S. Gov't bonds and notes, and undistributed profits of subsidiaries.
4. Balance of Payments Division, Department of Commerce.
5. Increase is indicated by (-).
6. Not available for years prior to 1960.
7. Seasonally adjusted annual rate, first six months, 1966.

called "compensating"). Autonomous transactions are assumed to be basic in the sense that they do not depend on the state of the balance of payments itself. The accommodating transactions are assumed to be the result of the autonomous transactions. Controversy over the basic balance concept has been excited primarily by the guesswork about the motives for transactions that must be indulged to dichotomize autonomous and compensating transactions. Autonomous (above the line) transactions are usually grouped to include trade in goods and services, private long-term capital movements (domestic and foreign), and government transactions (grants and capital except reserves). Accommodating (below the line) transactions are net movements of short-term capital and errors and omissions, the latter assumed to represent chiefly unrecorded short-term capital movements.

The balance on basic transactions is shown in Table 6, with Special Government Transactions and accommodating (below the line) transactions included. A similar pattern is described by the balance on basic transactions (line A) and the balance on basic and special Government transactions (line AA). Large deficits occurred in 1958 and 1959, followed by three years of improvements. The deterioration of the balance in 1963, followed by a substantial improvement in 1964, and deterioration again in 1965, shows a worsening condition of the basic balance because the year 1964 was atypical, as later sections will show.

The magnitude of the deficit was influenced profoundly in some years by Special Government Transactions (line 4). These transactions are movements of foreign official capital that result from U.S. Government negotiations to reduce the balance of payments impact of the U.S. foreign aid programs. Included in special transactions are advance repayments of U.S. Government loans, advances on military exports net, and sales of nonmarketable, medium-term, nonconvertible bonds denominated in foreign currencies ("Roosa bonds"). As a consequence of these special transactions, the balance on basic and special transactions showed a small surplus in 1961 and 1964.

Note that the accommodating or financing transactions, (lines 5 through 9) include U.S. private short-term capital and foreign commercial credits, recorded

TABLE 6

U.S. BALANCE OF INTERNATIONAL PAYMENTS,

BALANCE ON BASIC TRANSACTIONS BASIS, 1958-66

(Millions of Dollars)

	1958	1959	1960	1961	1962	1963	1964	1965	1966[8]	References, SCB, June, 1966: Table	Page	Line(s)
1. Balance on goods and services[1]	2206	147	4046	5621	5130	5897	8490	6957	----	1	25	24
2. U.S. Government grants and capital[2]	-3332	-2367	-3430	-2811	-2368	-3831	-4111	-3841	----	"	"	29+42-(43+44)+27+30+45+5B2[4]+57
3. Private long-term capital, U.S. and foreign[3]	-2545	-1574	-2081	-2092	-1745	-2959	-3805	-4403	-681	"	"	32-(38+40)-[50-(55+58+59)]
A. Balance on basic transactions basis	-3671	-3794	-1465	718	-1017	-893	574	-1287	----	----	----	----------
4. Special Government Transactions[5]	----	434	37	701	1402	617	328	528	----	----	----	----------
AA. Balance on basic and special Government transactions basis	-3671	-4228	-1502	17	-385	-1510	246	-1815	----	----	----	----------
5. U.S. private short-term capital, net	-311	-77	-1348	-1556	-544	-785	-2146	761	-14	1	25	38+40
6. U.S. foreign commercial credits	106	12	-90	175	-115	-23	113	146	46	"	"	55
7. Errors and omissions	511	423	-941	-1006	-1159	-352	-1011	-429	-228	"	"	60
8. U.S. liquid liabilities[6]	1073	2835	1738	1764	670	2292	2627	115	-346	"	"	58+59
9. U.S. monetary reserve assets[7]	2292	1035	2143	606	1533	378	171	1222	424	"	"	46

Source: Survey of Current Business, June, 1966. Table 1, pp.24-25, and Table 5, p.33. Compilation based on Report of the Review Committee for Balance of Payments Statistics. April, 1965. Table 9-2, p.105.

1. Excludes transfers under military grants
2. Includes private remittances and government pensions. Excludes military grants and advance prepayments of U.S. Gov't loans.
3. Excludes foreign holdings of U.S. bonds and notes, and undistributed profits of subsidiaries.
4. Table 5, p.33, line B2
5. Includes Advance repayments of U.S. Government loans,(Table 1, p.25, line 45) Advances on military exports net (Table 5, p.33, line B2), and Sales of nonmarketable, medium-term, nonconvertible securities,(Roosa Bonds) (Table 1, p.25, line 57)
6. Includes U.S. Government nonmarketable, medium-term, convertible securities.
7. Includes gold, convertible currencies, and IMF position. Reflects $259 million gold portion of increased U.S. IMF subscription in 1965. Increase indicated by (-).
8. First quarter, 1966, seasonally adjusted, SCB, June, 1966, Table 1, pp.28-29. Preliminary data.

and unrecorded (errors and omissions), U.S. liquid liabilities to all foreigners (official agencies, commercial banks, other foreign residents, and international and regional organizations), and U.S. official reserve assets (gold, convertible currencies, and the IMF gold tranche or automatic drawing rights).

The case for the basic balance basis of dividing international transactions rests on a substantial theoretical literature that supports the "autonomous" and "accommodating" dichotomy. In practice, the usefulness of the basic balance in tracing a country's external equilibrium position over long periods commends it. Recently the argument has been made by Hal Lary, formerly director of the Department of Commerce Balance of Payments Division and a long-time student of international monetary problems, that the "below the line" items in the basic balance (the short-term capital movements) are the transactions most readily affected by government policy, and in a world in which short-term capital is largely free to move among countries these transactions can be "accommodating" as defined in the theoretical literature.[45] The implication that monetary policy can, within the range of historical U.S. interest rate patterns, influence short-term capital movements in the magnitudes required to "accommodate" the "above the line" U.S. deficit of recent years must be greeted with doubt. As the previously cited Bernstein committee statement concluded, no single measure of the balance struck on international transactions is sufficient to represent the predicament faced by a country in its external monetary relationships.

<u>The Department of Commerce Liquidity Basis</u>. Since 1955 (until June, 1966) the Department of Commerce has adhered to a balance concept that reflects the net international liquidity position of the United States. The rationale for the selection of "below the line" transactions required by this balance is measurement of the resources available to U.S. monetary authorities to defend the dollar. Discussion of this controversial basis for the U.S. balance above cited its asymmetry and alleged inadequacies. It is prevented from fulfilling its purpose by the inclusion of some transactions not relevant to defense of the dollar and exclusion of others that are relevant. Table 7 shows the balance on liquidity basis with the "accommodating" transactions.

TABLE 7

U.S. BALANCE OF INTERNATIONAL PAYMENTS,

BALANCE ON LIQUIDITY BASIS, 1958-66

(Millions of Dollars)

	1958	1959	1960	1961	1962	1963	1964	1965	1966[1]	References, SCB, June, 1966: Table	Page	Line(s)
1. Balance on basic transactions (Table 5, line A)	-3671	-4228	-1502	17	-385	-1510	246	-1815	----	----	----	----
2. U.S. private short-term capital net	-311	-77	-1348	-1556	-544	-785	-2146	761	-14	1	25	38+40
3. U.S. foreign commercial credits	106	12	-90	175	-115	-23	113	146	46	"	"	55
4. Errors and omissions	511	423	-941	-1006	-1159	-352	-1011	-429	-228	"	"	60
5. Balance on BPD[2] liquidity basis	-3365	-3870	-3881	-2370	-2203	-2670	-2798	-1337	-1434	----	----	----
6. U.S. liquid liabilities[3]	1073	2835	1738	1764	670	2292	2627	115	450	"	"	58+59
7. U.S. monetary reserve assets[4]	2292	1035	2143	606	1533	378	171	1222	984	"	"	46

Source: Survey of Current Business, June, 1966, Table 1, pp.24-25, and Department of Commerce News Release, August 17, 1966,"U.S. Balance of Payments in Second Quarter 1966." Compilation based on Report of the Review Committee for Balance of Payments Statistics, April, 1965, Table 9.3, p.107.

1. Lines 2, 3, and 4, first quarter, 1966, seasonally adjusted preliminary data (Table 1, pp.28-29). Lines 5, 6, and 7, first half, 1966, seasonally adjusted annual rate.
2. Balance of Payments Division, Department of Commerce.
3. Includes U.S. Government nonmarketable, medium-term, convertible securities.
4. Includes gold, convertible currencies, and IMF position. Reflects $259 million gold portion of increased U.S. subscription to IMF in 1965. Increase is indicated by (-).

"Below the line" items include all liquid U.S. liabilities to foreigners, but only changes in the reserve assets of U.S. monetary authorities. This treatment of liquid capital is justified by the Department of Commerce on the grounds that the U.S. monetary authorities have no command of reserve-type assets other than their own holdings (because the U.S. does not exercise control over private foreign short-term assets), but must be prepared to meet, if necessary, the pressure on the dollar that would result if all foreign holdings of liquid assets in the United States were converted. These potentially disruptive foreign holdings are concentrated in bank deposits and short-term U.S. Government securities.

On a liquidity basis, the U.S. balance shows a larger deficit than on the basic transactions basis, for all years since 1959. However, the pattern in the liquidity basis balance is a general decline in the deficit excepting the large deficits of 1963 and 1964 attributable to abrupt increases in U.S. liquid liabilities. On a basic transactions basis (line 1) 1964 was a year of remarkable improvement in the deficit; on a liquidity basis 1964 was a year of deterioration.

The Bernstein committee concluded that the balance on a liquidity basis did not provide the "most useful" summary of the over-all U.S. payments position and stated its objection:[46]

> The BPD concept draws too sharp and artificial a distinction between private foreigners and private U.S. residents, and it fails to distinguish between private foreigners and foreign monetary authorities. It implies that U.S. reserve assets are needed to protect the dollar only against withdrawals of foreign holdings, whereas historical experience demonstrates that outflows of domestic capital typically play a leading role in payments deficits and speculative runs on a currency. On the other hand, the BPD concept implies that all foreign holdings represent an equal threat to the reserves, whereas in fact only foreign monetary authorities can directly draw down U.S. reserves. Thus, the BPD concept is either

too narrow or too broad, depending upon the perspective from which it is viewed.

In place of the net international liquidity balance used by the Department of Commerce, the Committee recommended "a summary presentation of the balance of payments in which settlement items, regarded as financing the balance on all other transactions, include only 'reserve transactions' and, when appropriate, special intergovernmental transactions."[47] The Committee defined its objective to be the measurement of the gap between the normal supply of and demand for foreign exchange, a gap that would require drawing down the supply of U.S. reserve assets if the variation in the exchange position of the dollar was to be held within the IMF limits. It remains to be seen whether "normal" will be a standard any less difficult to apply than the other adjectives that have perplexed students of the balance of payments, for example, "basic," "liquid," "autonomous," and "accommodating."

Table 8 shows the balance on an official reserve transactions basis, the measure added to the Department of Commerce reserve position summary table in mid-1966. With minor exceptions the Bernstein Committee recommendations were accepted in striking the new balance. Official reserve transactions include changes in U.S. official reserve assets (gold and convertible foreign currencies) and changes in liquid and certain nonliquid liabilities to foreign official agencies (including the IMF). The balance on official transactions basis is similar in most respects to the balance on liquidity; but the transactions below the line in the official transactions basis include (in addition to changes in official reserve assets) liquid and some nonliquid liabilities only to foreign official agencies. Only in 1962 is the balance on official transactions basis larger than the balance on liquidity. Since 1962 (and, if that year is excluded, since 1960) the official transactions deficit has been declining. Unlike the liquidity balance which probably reaches equilibrium at a deficit of $500 to $800 million, the official transactions deficit reaches equilibrium at zero.

Analysis of Balance of Payments Data

A country's position in the international economy

TABLE 8

U.S. BALANCE OF INTERNATIONAL PAYMENTS,

BALANCE ON OFFICIAL RESERVE TRANSACTIONS BASIS, 1958-66

(Millions of Dollars)

	1958	1959	1960	1961	1962	1963	1964	1965	1966[1]	References, SCB, June, 1966: Table	Page	Line(s)
1. Balance on basic transactions (Table 5, line A)	-3671	-4228	-1502	17	-385	-1510	246	-1815	----	----	----	----
2. U.S. private short-term capital net	-311	-77	-1348	-1556	-544	-785	-2146	761	-14	1	25	38+40
3. Foreign commercial credits	106	12	-90	175	-115	-23	113	146	46	"	"	55
4. Errors and omissions	511	423	-941	-1006	-1159	-352	-1011	-429	-228	"	"	60
5. Foreign private short-term capital other than commercial credits	----	----	289	1083	213	619	1554	132	----	7	35	1-2
6. Foreign holdings of U.S. Government bonds and notes, except official monetary institutions[2]	----	----	----	----	254	-16	154	138	-18	3	30	20
7. Foreign official short-term capital, except official monetary institutions	----	----	----	----	----	9	148	-38	47	"	"	19
8. Balance on official reserve transaction basis	----	----	-3402	-1347	-2706	-2044	-1546	-1305	-874	"	"	13
9. U.S. official reserve[3] assets	2292	1035	2143	606	1533	378	171	1222	984	3 1	30 25	16 46
10. Liquid liabilities to foreign official agencies	----	----	1259	741	919	1673	1073	-17	110	3	30	17
11. Certain nonliquid[3] liabilities to foreign official agencies	----	----	----	----	254	-7	302	100		"	"	18

Source: Survey of Current Business, June, 1966, Table 1, pp.24-25, Table 3, p.30, and Table 7, p.35, and Department of Commerce News Release, August 17, 1966,"U.S. Balance of Payments in Second Quarter 1966." Compilation based on Report of the Review Committee for Balance of Payments Statistics, April, 1965, Table 9.1, p.104, and Table 9.5, p.110.

1. Lines 1-7, first quarter, 1966, seasonally adjusted annual rate. Preliminary data, lines 8-11, first half, 1966, seasonally adjusted annual rate, Department of Commerce News Release August 17, 1966.
2. Increase indicated by (-).
3. Increase indicated by (-). Reflects $259 million payment of gold portion of increased U.S. subscription to IMF in 1965.

can be represented by any of several balance concepts, as shown in preceding sections. None of the balances has a claim to general superiority over the others; each has its own advantages depending on the purpose for which the balance is struck. The basic balance concepts are preferred for comparisons among countries and for analyses that cover long periods of time. Official transactions concepts are preferred for gauging the "exposure" of a key currency country under fixed exchange rates. The particular balance struck, however--regardless of its appropriateness--discloses nothing about the fundamental forces that produced it. When the question shifts from "What is country A's balance?" to "Why is country A's balance in deficit?," the activity shifts from accounting to analysis. The United States has had a deficit on its official transactions balance each year since 1960, a fact observable in the country's external accounts. But the underlying causes of the deficits (and the guidelines to policy actions that might diminish or eliminate the deficit) are discernible only from analysis of differences among countries with respect to economic growth rates, interest rate levels, economic fluctuations, exchange rates, and other factors.

DEFINING THE PROBLEM

The United States has had a deficit balance on liquidity transactions during each of the last fifteen years except 1957, but the "problem" of the deficit has engaged the American financial community and the U.S. Government for only about six years. During most of the postwar years through the late 1950's, the deficit balance in the U.S. international accounts was regarded as a desirable condition and U.S. economic foreign policy was framed with the intent to continue the deficit. What circumstances caused the United States to change its mind about its external balance about 1960? The appearance of Europe (the Common Market) as a competitor was probably exaggerated, but it was highly important. More important to the Kennedy Administration were the constraints imposed by the balance of payments deficit on fiscal and monetary policies to stimulate the economy. Other factors included pride, the symbolism of gold, and confusion about the basic causes of the deficit.

Recovery of Western Europe

Few observers in 1956 or 1957 would have predicted that the next two years would see a return of Western Europe's economic power. The economic recovery of Western Europe and the passing of dollar scarcity--the barriers to convertibility--were not anticipated in the United States although American foreign policy had been framed for ten years with the intent of bringing about these developments. When the liquidity basis balance swung against the United States in 1958 by a magnitude of nearly $4 billion (from a surplus of $.6 billion in 1957, occasioned by the Suez Crisis, to a deficit of $3.4 billion in 1958), the Treasury Department and the Congress became exercised. The persistence of deficits approximating $3.9 billion in 1959 and 1960, nearly half settled by sale of U.S. gold reserve assets, confirmed the urgency of the balance of payments situation; and the public became aware of the shift of fortune that had taken place in U.S. international economic relations. The confirmation that the large American deficit balance was other than a transitory aberration and the decline of confidence in the dollar in Western Europe, indicated by a run on gold in the fall of 1960, kindled resentment in the United States against France and West Germany. Gaullism especially stirred American indignation, the predilection of the French for such ventures in economic foreign policy--undervaluation of the franc in 1926, refusal of support for the Kredit Anstalt in 1929, and administration of the coup de grace to the pound in 1931--having apparently been forgotten.

The Flagging U.S. Economy

Coincident with the aggravation of the deficit in 1959 and 1960, the U.S. economy entered a period of faltering recovery that ended in a recession. A mere twenty-five months had elapsed between the trough of the 1957-58 contraction and the peak of the 1960 expansion. Unemployment reached 6.8 percent in 1958 and remained at 5.5 percent or greater until 1963. Economic growth had become an important national problem by 1960, and it was an issue in the presidential election. The constraint imposed by the deficit balance on the type of policies that the government could employ, and the range over which policies could be varied, has been cited in a number of studies as the most aggravating effect of the balance of payments deficit.[48]

Other Factors

A country's regard for its money is imbued with an emotional quality that has no basis in reason, but it weighs in the problem all the same. The British romance with the pound has, at times in the past, justified over-valuation in the British mind. Certainly, the pressure on the dollar's value in the foreign exchange markets was an assault on American pride; and every avenue for possible restoration of the "good as gold" dollar was potentially open to pursuit. Foreign aid, the factor presumed responsible for the deficit, was perhaps most vulnerable of all. A quick and decisive solution to the deficit was much desired in the early 1960's.

There was considerable confusion about the reasons for the deficit in the first recognition of its problem character. It was alleged that the American economy was unduly inflationary, no longer competitive, the scorn of presumably sound European banking judgment, and similar generalities. Not unexpectedly, the effort to formulate a concensus on a proper policy was both slow and tortuous.

Notes to Chapter 4

1. Richard N. Gardner, Sterling-Dollar Diplomacy (Oxford: The Clarendon Press, 1956), p.287.

2. International Bank for Reconstruction and Development, Second Annual Report of the Executive Directors (Washington: 1947), p.17.

3. Ibid., p.23.

4. The Cominform, centered at Belgrade, was established to exchange information among Communist Parties in the various countries of the world and to coordinate their activities.

5. Convertibility of the pound was suspended after five weeks of nearly disastrous experience in which about $1 billion of reserves were lost (July 15 to August 20, 1947). Sterling Area debts of Great Britain were not cut back, as agreed at the time of the British loan, nor were nondiscrimination promises kept because of dollar scarcity. See Gardner, op.cit., pp.306-47, for

a discussion of the inept diplomacy that produced and followed the 1946 loan agreement.

6. Delivered at the Harvard University commencement on June 5, 1947. New York Times, June 6, 1947.

7. Title I of the Foreign Assistance Act of 1948. Other titles provided economic cooperation assistance to China and U.S.-occupied areas.

8. Commission on Foreign Economic Policy, Staff Papers Presented to the Commission on Foreign Economic Policy (Washington: Government Printing Office, 1954), p.28.

9. Ibid., p.27.

10. Forerunner of the nineteen-member Organization for European Economic Cooperation (OEEC) organized by ERP recipients in 1948.

11. References for extended discussion of these early exercises in European monetary cooperation are Scammell, op.cit., and Robert Triffin, Europe and the Money Muddle (New Haven: Yale University Press, 1957).

12. A system of monthly forecasts and end-of-month settlements was established. See Scammell, op.cit., pp.281-82.

13. Triffin, op.cit., pp.54-55, 160.

14. A complex system of shares or tranches governed the gold-dollar EPU credit proportions. See Scammell, op.cit., pp.290-95.

15. Commission on Foreign Economic Policy, op.cit., p.15. Scammell argues that the dollar scarcity gap was significantly less than this estimate. Scammell, op.cit., p.330 ff.

16. Ibid., p.15.

17. This table presents a "basic" transactions balance for the years after 1957 that is not strictly comparable with data for earlier years. The data are included to show the substantial shift in flows of funds that took

place during the seventeen-year period.

18. A large segment of informed opinion, especially in Great Britain, presumed that the dollar scarcity problem had become a permanent fixture of international monetary relations. See Thomas Balogh, "The United States and International Economic Equilibrium," in Foreign Economic Policy for the United States, Editor Seymour E. Harris (Cambridge, Mass.: Harvard University Press, 1948); John H. Williams, Economic Stability in the Modern World (London: Athcone Press, 1952); and Sir Dennis H. Robertson, Britain in the World Economy (London: Allen and Unwin, 1954).

19. Convertibility refers in this discussion to the technical definition imposed by IMF Articles of Agreement Article VIII, Section 4. In general, this requires a country to buy balances of its currency held by another member, the buying member having the option to pay in the currency of the member offering balances for payment or gold. Convertible currencies are defined in Article XIX, paragraph (d) as "currencies of.....members which are not availing themselves of the transitional (discrimination) arrangements under Article XIV, Section 2, together with its holdings of the currencies of such non-members as the Fund may from time to time specify. The term currency for this purpose includes without limitation coins, paper money, bank balances, bank acceptances, and government obligations issued with a maturity not exceeding twelve months."

20. Britain's respect for the Articles of the IMF was open to question because of the cursory notification she gave of an intention to devalue.

21. France was ruled ineligible to use IMF borrowing facilities because she violated the Articles of Agreement with her devaluation of 1948 that established multiple exchange rates. The ineligibility ruling was lifted in 1954.

22. West Germany's progress from a position as the EPU's largest debtor in 1950-51 to the largest creditor after 1954 and France's 1951 surplus that gave way to persistent deficits until 1959, only to be followed in turn by massive reserve accumulations, are examples of

these wide swings in external positions.

23. The 1955 renewal agreement had provided for termination of the Union when countries holding 50 percent of EPU quotas announced their desire to make their currencies convertible outside the Union (OEEC) area.

24. Scammell, _op.cit._, pp.177-83.

25. _Ibid._, pp.311-12.

26. Organization for European Economic Cooperation, _Statistics of National Product and Expenditure_ (Paris: OEEC, 1954), p.30.

27. Gross Domestic Product. Cf. United Nations, _The Growth of World Industry, 1938-61, International Analysis and Tables_ (United Nations: 1965), p.150.

28. The origin and development of the idea of European unity in the period since 1945 are traced in Max Beloff, _The United States and the Unity of Europe_ (Washington: The Brookings Institution, 1963).

29. _Ibid_, p.1

30. _Ibid_.

31. _Ibid_., pp.14-20.

32. _Ibid_., p.52.

33. Considerable difficulty was experienced in deciding on the breadth of membership in the proposed union, both in early State Department planning and the American Committee's early efforts; should the union be European--i.e., embrace the Satellite countries and, possibly, the Soviet Union--or should it be Western European, Continental European, or Atlantic? See Beloff, _op.cit._, pp.49-75.

34. The EDC never came into existence because of the failure of France to ratify the treaty in 1954.

35. The Treaty of Rome itself was devoid of threats

to exporting countries. American observers had followed the progress of the treaty from the Spaak report until ratification and made U.S. preferences known to the negotiators.

36. This argument and the options of the United States are discussed at length in a series of papers prepared for the subcommittee on International Exchange and Payments of the Joint Economic Committee in a report entitled, Factors Affecting the United States Balance of Payments (Washington: Government Printing Office, 1962). See especially Irwin B. Kravis, "The U.S. Trade Position and the Common Market," pp.87-104.

37. Ibid., Walther Lederer, "Measuring the Balance of Payments," p.82.

38. See Lary, op.cit.; Fritz Machlup, International Payments, Debts and Gold (New York: Charles Scribner's Sons, 1964), pp.140-66; and Walter S. Salant, et.al., The United States Balance of Payments in 1968 (Washington The Brookings Institution, 1963), pp.2-23.

39. Review Committee for Balance of Payments Statistics, The Balance of Payments Statistics of the United States (Washington: Government Printing Office, 1965). The report of the Review Committee has itself enjoyed some review. See Joint Economic Committee, The Balance of Payments Statistics (Washington: Government Printing Office, 1965),"Hearings before the Subcommittee on Economic Statistics," Part 3, June 9, 1965.

40. Ibid., p.2.

41. Ibid.

42. Ibid., p.3.

43. Ibid.

44. Edward M. Bernstein, "A Supplementary Note on the Balance of Payments Statistics," in Joint Economic Committee, The Balance of Payments Statistics (Washington: Government Printing Office, 1965), p.289.

45. Lary, op.cit., pp.148-50.

46. The Review Committee for Balance of Payments Statistics, *op.cit.*, p.109.

47. *Ibid.*, p.109.

48. Lary, *op.cit.*, p.6, and Salant, *op.cit.*, p.2.

CHAPTER 5 A POLICY-MIX FOR EXTERNAL EQUILIBRIUM

FORMULATING A BALANCE OF PAYMENTS POLICY

The actions taken by the U.S. Government to deal with the balance of payments deficit, after its problem character first became apparent in 1959, were simple and direct. Development loans, which recipients had been free to spend wherever they wished, were tied to expenditure in the United States. Military procurement procedures were reviewed to save foreign exchange. Duty-free allowances on tourist purchases abroad were cut. Dependents of overseas military personnel were threatened with repatriation. As the gross difficulties associated with eliminating the deficit became apparent, policies that worked indirectly were adopted. The most important of these policies involved promotion of exports through liberalization of export financing, through increased attention to world trade fairs, and by improvement of consular facilities.

The large U.S. gold reserve--over $20 billion in 1958, representing more than half the world supply[1]--and the fact that the beneficiaries of the U.S. payments deficit were countries in Western Europe combined, temporarily, to give the administration some advantages in coping with the deficit. Having large reserves, the U.S. could take the time required to formulate appropriate actions with respect to the balance of payments. As the policy and the instruments of its implementation took shape, moreover, the administration could count on a large measure of cooperation from the nation's creditors--the Western European countries--because of past U.S. aid to these countries. An initial skepticism about the wisdom of U.S. balance of payments policies soon turned to criticism. Nonetheless, the time margin required by the United States to plan balance of payments policies, to introduce gradually more potent policies, and to monitor the effects of the prevailing policy-mix was a safeguard against summary actions that might have upset the whole international payments system.

Constraints on U.S. Balance of Payments Policy

The range of policies that the U.S. Government was free to consider, as it moved to correct unusually large deficits that were recorded in the years 1958-60, was restricted by the importance that the dollar had achieved as a key currency in international economic affairs. Most important was the widespread use of the dollar as a reserve currency. Central banks held a part of their monetary reserves in dollar claims. Since only official agencies could buy gold from the United States in trade for dollars, and tradition required many central banks to hold a fixed proportion of their reserves in gold, the reserve currency status of the dollar had great significance for balance of payments policy. In addition to being a reserve currency, the dollar had become the currency in which international and interregional transactions were most often settled and regional monetary agencies kept their accounts. Large dollar balances were held by individuals, commercial banks, and other financial institutions throughout the world. Therefore, the dollar was constantly scrutinized by these holders for evidence of any change that might diminish its exchange value.

The key currency status of the dollar reflects an international banking service that is performed by the United States for the countries of the world. It is not a status that was sought as a matter of national policy, but a greatness that was thrust upon the dollar as a consequence of its unrivaled strength in the postwar period. There was no expectation at the Bretton Woods conference that the dollar would be the postwar key currency. As a key currency the dollar performed its role without adverse effects on the U.S. external position until the convertibility of European currencies was accomplished in 1958. Thereafter, with mounting U.S. payments deficits, the key currency status of the dollar had the effect of aggravating speculative pressures against it and limiting the policy options that the U.S. Government might invoke to correct the external imbalance. The incompatibility of the key currency status and the Bretton Woods system precluded the U.S. availing itself of the adjustment mechanism provided for in the system. Because the dollar was the international accounting unit, it was forced to maintain a fixed exchange relationship to gold and other convertible currencies. Professor Halm has summarized the predicament faced by the U.S. at the close of the 1950's:[2]

> Two problems must be faced. We must become aware of the fact that a key currency country is in a more sensitive payments position than other countries simply because it has taken it upon itself to convert, on demand, foreign exchange reserves of the "member" countries into gold or commodities. While this obligation may not be serious under normal conditions and with the cooperation of all "members," it could become dangerous for both the key country and the "members" if a general desire to convert the key currency into gold were to lead to a sudden collapse of international liquidity.
>
> The second problem concerns the restriction which the key currency country suffers as a result of the service it renders to the international community: It may not, as the "members" are permitted to, devalue its currency and it cannot always follow the domestic economic policy which would be best if its responsibilities as (a) key currency country could be disregarded.

As a practical matter, the restriction of U.S. domestic economic policy because of the key currency status of the dollar was more important than inability to devalue. After France devalued in 1958, the major world currencies entered a period of relative stability; and the U.S. would probably not have considered devaluation seriously even had the dollar not enjoyed key currency status.

As the U.S. imbalance appeared in 1960, the third successive year of deficits approaching $4 billion and gold losses averaging $1.8 billion, official policy-making was forced to emphasize short-term actions which might quickly reduce the deficit. During the year 1959 the U.S. merchandise surplus had declined sharply, after a promising upward trend at mid-year. Export promotion, liberalization of export credit programs, and an economic recovery in Europe had induced a large expansion in exports during 1960 and quieted some of the fears that the U.S. economy had lost its competitive position in foreign markets. Despite highly favorable results in the merchandise account, however, the deficit on a liquidity basis increased. A new element--capital outflow--had arisen to offset the merchandise export increase.

The detail of the foreign balance for the five years 1957-61 is presented in Table 9. In the years 1958 and 1959 the balance on goods and services (line 1) declined rapidly, resulting in negative balances on goods and services and unilateral transfers. Beginning in 1960, an increase in the current account balance from $2,121 million to $7,086 million in 1961 resulted in a goods and services balance--including unilateral transfers--of $1,684 million in 1960 and $3,035 million in 1961. The persistence of the deficit in 1960 and 1961 despite large increases in the merchandise trade balance was attributable to net outflows of U.S. private capital (recorded <u>and</u> unrecorded) and to that portion of U.S. Government grants and capital that had a net payments effect on the balance, about one-third in 1960 and one-quarter in 1961.

U.S. deficits shown in the years after 1957 were settled to an increasing extent by gold sales. The significance of gold losses was at least partly its emotional impact; despite heavy sales the U.S. share of the world[3] gold stock was about 41 percent in 1961. In 1958, however, the U.S. share had been 52 percent. U.S. gold reserve losses were matched by gold reserve gains in a relatively small number of European countries[4] which historically have held a high proportion of their reserves in the form of gold. The proportion of their reserve increases that these countries chose to accumulate in the form of gold (in contrast to dollars and other convertible currencies), given the increase in world gold supplies from new production and Soviet gold sales, defined an upper limit of the deficit that the U.S. might incur, on the average, without loss of gold reserves. This limit has been hypothesized by Høst-Madsen as two-thirds of the increase in world gold supplies, and the gold loss from deficits beyond this limit would approximate 60 percent of the above-limit amounts; on the liquidity transactions definition

TABLE 9

U.S. BALANCE OF PAYMENTS AND RESERVE POSITION, 1957-61
(Millions of Dollars)

	1957	1958	1959	1960	1961
1. Balance on goods and services[1]	5,729	2,206	147	4,046	5,621
2. Balance on goods and services and unilateral transfers[1]	3,384	-155	-2,301	1,684	3,035
3. Balance on private capital	-2,445	-1,677	1,196	-1,781	-1,709
A. U.S. capital[2]	-3,577	-2,936	-2,375	-3,885	-4,180
(a) Short-term	-276	-311	-77	-1,348	-1,246
(b) Long-term	-3,301	-2,625	-2,298	-2,537	-2,934
B. Foreign capital[2]	1,132	1,259	3,571	2,104	2,471
(a) Short-term	681	1,179	3,115	1,648	1,939
(b) Long-term and direct	451	80	456	456	532
4. U.S. Government capital	-958	-971	-353	-1,105	-926
5. Errors and omissions	1,184	511	423	-941	-1,006
6. Reserve gold assets transactions[3]	-1,165	2,292	1,035	2,143	606
7. Balance on liquidity transactions[4]	578	-3,365	-3,870	-3,881	-2,370

Source: Survey of Current Business, June, 1966. Table 1, pp.24-25, and Table 3, pp.30-31; and, Department of Commerce News Release, August 17, 1966, "U.S. Balance of Payments in Second Quarter 1966."

1. Excludes military grants.
2. (-) Indicates outflow.
3. (-) Indicates increase in reserve assets (gold, convertible currencies, and gold tranche position, IMF).
4. Derived 1 plus U.S. grants and capital (Chapter 4, Table 7) plus (3A(b)-3B(b)) plus 3A(a) plus foreign commercial credits (Chapter 4, Table 7) plus 5.

of the deficit, according to Høst Madsen, the U.S. could have expected to suffer no gold losses during the 1958-63 period with deficits up to $1 billion.[5]

Regressions computed by the author for annual data 1950-65 and quarterly data 1960-66, relating U.S. gold sales to the payments deficit, are given in Table 10.

TABLE 10

THE U.S. DEFICIT AND GOLD LOSSES, 1950-66 (Millions of Dollars)

Data	Equation[1]	$S_{y.x}$	r_{xy}	Deficit for Zero Gold Loss
	1950-65			
Annual; liquidity concept of deficit	$Y=-364+.51X$	566	.751	713
"	$Y=-366+.51X+.00001X^2$	574	.751	714
	1960-66[2]			
Quarterly, seasonally adjusted; official transactions concept of deficit	$Y=182-.35X+.0005X^2$	235	.508	621
Same; deficit lagged one quarter	$Y=117+.36X-.00015X^2$	261	.332	224
Same; deficit lagged two quarters	$Y=53+1.04X-.00083X^2$	241	.535	-
Same; deficit lagged three quarters	$Y=86+.75X-.0006X^2$	260	.390	-

Source: Survey of Current Business, June, 1966, Table 1, pp.25-26, and Table 3, pp.30-31.

1. "X" variable is U.S. deficit, on a liquidity concept basis for annual data, on an official transactions basis for quarterly data. $S_{y.x}$ is the standard error of the prediction. Standard error indicates size of estimating error on average; the odds are 20 to 1 that the error will be less than 1.96 times the standard error. The standard error is $S_{y.xx^2}$ for quadratic equations. The "r" value (correlation coefficient) measures the relationship between X(U.S. deficit) and Y(gold loss), and r^2 gives the proportion of total variance in gold loss "explained" by the deficit.

2. Data extend from first quarter, 1960, through first quarter, 1966.

The data indicate that, on average, a deficit of about $710 million could have been incurred annually throughout the period 1950-65 without a gold loss. Allowing for annual additions to the world gold supply of $500 million, and assuming that the high reserve countries maintain a ratio of 3:2, gold to dollar reserves, the U.S. deficit on average could have approximated $1.1 billion ($710 million + .60x$500 million) without a loss of U.S. gold. The regression equations based on quarterly data presented in Table 10 indicate a low degree of reliability. Note, however, that the correlation increases as the deficit variable is lagged two periods. Since the official transactions deficit concept data are available only for years 1960 and after, a regression equation fitted to annual data would have no prediction reliability.

Policy Options To Correct the Deficit

The courses of action that the U.S. Government was free to consider as it moved to formulate a balance of payments policy were a relatively small subset of the wide-ranging suggestions offered, and sometimes pressed, by the diverse group of Americans and foreigners who spoke out on the problem.[6] Some actions had already been taken by 1961--tying of purchases financed by foreign aid, shifting of off-shore procurement away from countries with which the U.S. was running a deficit balance, and liberalization of export financing--and their expansion would have little effect on the balance. The responsibilities imposed by the key currency status of the dollar further limited the actions that could be seriously considered. Most important, from the standpoint of restricting the range of "available" policy options, were the domestic goals that had been established for the American economy. After six years of underemployed resources, and the experience of two economic contractions in the three-year period 1957-60, contractionist fiscal and monetary policies--favorite European remedies for external deficits--were neither economically justified nor politically practical. Domestic policies to aid the balance of payments would have to emphasize the positive (productivity-promoting investment and full utilization of capacity) rather than succumb to the negative (deflation of wages and prices). Generally stated, the U.S. balance of payments policies would have to be formulated in the context of expansionist domestic policies, a course which, according to orthodox prescriptions for redressing an external imbalance, was inherently contradictory.[7]

The extensive literature that was directed to the problem of the U.S. external balance and restoration of equilibrium will not be summarized here.[8] A concensus had arisen at the end of 1960 that a balance of payments policy was essential to the American economy, that expansionist policies in the domestic economy should continue, that ad hoc policy actions already taken were inadequate to redress the imbalance, and that further policy actions should operate on the external sector. Removal of the domestic policy actions from the fixed balance of payments policy options left a range of possibilities that still required narrowing. One possibility, import restrictions, was generally eliminated as an undesirable choice despite pressure from protectionists to whom the deficit offered an opportunity to associate their perennial cause with the country's welfare. Foreign aid reductions were similarly rejected, largely because the impact of foreign aid on the deficit had been reduced to a relatively small payments amount, but also because of a conviction, widely held, that the implements of foreign policy should not be employed solely for balance of payments purposes.

The President's Message of February 6, 1961

A message sent to the Congress by President Kennedy on February 6, 1961, defined the framework of an external economic policy for the U.S. in terms of the consensus that had emerged during the preceding three years.[9] The message cited the gold outflow of the past three years as the element which had focused attention on a problem that had smoldered for more than a decade, disguised by willingness of foreign official agencies to accumulate dollar claims as reserves. Henceforth, however, the U.S. would have to "take its balance of payments into account when formulating its economic policies and conducting its economic affairs."[10] Economic progress in the United States was held to be the basis for economic strength abroad. In the language of the message, "Accordingly, the first requirement for restoring balance in our international payments is to take all possible steps to insure the effective performance of our own economic system--to improve our technology, lower our production and marketing costs, and devise new and superior products, under conditions of price stability."[11] The "problem" character of the deficit was defined by the President in such a way as to obviate any implication that U.S. unilateral transfers should be reduced: "The surplus of our exports over imports, while substantial, has not been large enough to cover our expenditures for United States establishments abroad, for capital invested abroad by private American businesses, and for government economic assistance and loan programs. All of these outlays are essential."[12] It was clear from the message that the President was counting on an increasing American export strength to counter future payments pressures.

The President's message concluded with a statement of principles that underlay American foreign economic policy, following which he proposed a program of action conceived in part to help the country meet short-term reserve drains and in part to correct the basic deficit. Because the principles stated by the President continue to provide the bases for American policies, they are quoted in full:[13]

> 1. The United States official dollar price of gold can and will be maintained at $35 an ounce. Exchange controls over trade and investment will not be invoked. Our national security and economic assistance programs will be carried forward. Those who fear weakness in the dollar will find their fears unfounded. Those who hope for speculative reasons for an increase in the price of gold will find their hopes in vain.
>
> 2. We must now gain control of our balance-of-payments position so that we can achieve over-all equilibrium in our international payments. This means that any sustained future outflow of dollars into the monetary reserves of other countries should come about only as the result of considered judgments as to the appropriate needs for dollar reserves.
>
> 3. In seeking over-all equilibrium we must place maximum emphasis on expanding our exports.

Our costs and prices must therefore be kept low; and the government must play a more vigorous part in helping to enlarge foreign markets for American goods and services.

4. A return to protectionism is not a solution. Such a course would provoke retaliation; and the balance of trade, which is now substantially in our favor, could be turned against us with disastrous effects on the dollar.

5. The flow of resources from the industrialized countries to the developing countries must be increased. In all that we do to strengthen our balance of payments, we must be especially mindful that the less developed countries remain in a weak financial position. Help from the industrialized countries is more important than ever; we cannot strengthen our balance of payments at the expense of the developing countries without incurring even greater dangers to our national security.

6. The United States must take the lead in harmonizing the financial and economic policies for growth and stability of those industrialized nations of the world whose economic behavior significantly influences the course of the world economy and the trend of international payments.

The action program proposed by the President was divided into two parts. Part One, measures to ease the short-term demand for U.S. reserves by surplus countries, included four proposals: (1) a proposal to improve international monetary institutions; (2) a proposal to use American drawing rights in the International Monetary Fund; (3) proposals to increase interest rates payable on time and savings deposits held in this country by foreign governments or monetary authorities, and to exempt from tax income accruing to foreign central banks from U.S. Government securities (the Treasury Department would also issue securities at special rates of interest for holding by foreign governments or monetary authorities); and, (4) a proposal to forbid the holding of gold abroad by Americans.

These proposals were designed to stem the repatriation of foreign funds and reduce gold sales by increasing the appeal of American short-term investments to foreign official agencies and by curbing speculation against the dollar in the gold markets by Americans. For the longer term, the intention of the United States to exercise its IMF drawing privileges was declared, and cooperative efforts to increase the reserve-enforcing lending facilities of the IMF were solicited. The restrained nature of these proposals, considering the magnitude of U.S. capital outflow and its contribution to the deficit, indicates a preference by the administration for policies that could be progressively strengthened if the balance of payments deficit required.

Part Two of the action program, designed to relieve the basic deficit (i.e., the imbalance on merchandise and long-term capital account), contained fourteen proposals: (1) a proposal to approve U.S. membership in the OECD; (2) a proposal to extend and improve commercial attachés and trade missions abroad; (3) a proposal for an Advisory Commission on Labor and Management Policy to encourage productivity gains, advance automation, and encourage wage and price stability; (4) a proposal to liberalize Export-Import Bank financing programs to place American export financing facilities on a par with foreign facilities; (5) a proposal to promote foreign travel in the U.S.; (6) a proposal to seek increases in agricultural exports; (7) an affirmation that the tying of U.S. economic assistance be continued; (8) a proposal to press for the removal of quota and tariff discrimination against U.S. exports; (9) a proposal to press surplus countries to eliminate the restrictions that still remain limiting the opportunities for their citizens to invest in the United States; (10) a proposal to remove any special, preferential tax treatment of American capital invested abroad, if such treatment is reported to exist; (11) a solicitation of contributions for foreign assistance to less developed countries and for common defense by industrialized countries whose economic and financial positions permit; (12) a proposal to reduce to $100 the duty-free allowance applicable to imports by American tourists; (13) a proposal to centralize in the Bureau of the

Budget the review of foreign exchange spending by U.S. Government agencies; and, (14) a proposal to substitute for the policy of repatriation of military dependents a reduction of tourism and consumer goods purchases by military personnel abroad.

These proposals continued some policies already in operation, but attempted also to strengthen them; for example, export promotion, efforts to maintain price stability, tying of economic assistance, and foreign tourism in the U.S. Some proposals could not be implemented unilaterally; for example, foreign discrimination against U.S. exports, foreign investment in the U.S., and foreign assistance and defense contributions. Other proposals would have an unknown effect on the balance of payments until departmental studies disclosed their relationship to the balance; these included the expansion of agricultural exports and the elimination of tax havens. As in the short-term proposals, the long-term basic balance measures could, in many cases, be imposed with gradually increasing effect if balance of payments developments required.

After three years of serious balance of payments deficits, and wholly inadequate and inarticulated policies to deal with them, a vigorous beginning had been made. Short-term and long-term measures had been proposed, a recognition that the problem of external imbalance was both acute and, in its basic manifestations, of indefinite duration. The European countries would be joined by the United States in the OECD, possibly the first step toward the achievement of an Atlantic community. If any important criticism of the program were to be made, it would be the underestimation--as in the short-term proposals--of the disturbing effect of capital movements (in this case, long-term capital on the U.S. external balance). However, the proposals that related to capital movements shared in common with the other proposals a mildness in initial application which was, for initial prescriptions with unknown results, a wise policy formulation. The policy-mix reflected the main stream of economic theory, ignoring the controversial and the untried options that had proliferated since the balance of payments problem attained serious proportions. Within the year, a substantial part of the program was approved by the Congress.

The Federal Reserve System and Balance of Payments Policy

Monetary authorities historically have claimed the responsibility for managing the external value of their country's money. In the United States, this prescription has, since the mid-1930's, required the dollar's value to be stabilized at one-thirty-fifth ounce of gold. From the mid-1930's until March, 1961, however, the external value of the dollar had been maintained without resort to foreign exchange operations by U.S. monetary authorities. Beginning in March, 1961, the U.S. Treasury, acting through the Federal Reserve Bank of New York, began entering into foreign exchange transactions for the purpose of countering speculative pressures against the dollar in foreign exchange markets. Underlying this new venture by the United States was a carefully contrived partnership with leading central banks to provide a greater degree of stability for key currencies under the Bretton Woods system of fixed exchange rates. The American balance of payments policy became heavily dependent upon this informal partnership that brought the monetary authorities of leading nations together monthly[14] and, on an ad hoc basis, at other times dictated by existing or emerging international monetary problems.

The objectives of the Treasury in its foreign exchange operations were described in 1962 by Under Secretary of the Treasury Robert V. Roosa as follows:[15]

> Our foreign-exchange operations have so far been mainly designed to help in providing a breathing space during which these basic programs (the program contained in the President's Special Message of February 6, 1961) could have a chance to be effective. In our judgment, they have been most helpful in deterring unwarranted speculation and unwanted capital flows, and in reducing the drain on our gold stock, which stands as the bulwark of the whole international currency system.
>
> Some minor limited selling operations in the spot market have been undertaken more

> recently to alleviate temporary pressures, using foreign exchange acquired by borrowing in Switzerland and Italy (or limited amounts acquired at times when the rate would not be adversely affected). Operations have been mainly concentrated, however, in forward exchange. These markets can at times be quite thin and even a relatively limited volume of market demand can have an excessive impact on rates, which are not subject to limitations under IMF regulations but which can generate great pressures upon the spot rates. When the forward rate, whether because of expectations concerning future currency values or for other reasons, moves conspicuously out of line with its interest parity, short-term private capital movements can be set off that may be disturbing to both the country receiving and the country losing funds. It is useful to have facilities for testing out whether the particular developments are in fact deeply rooted and sustained, or whether they are short-lived and may soon be reversed.

It has been common practice for most countries in Western Europe to intervene in the foreign exchange markets to maintain the value of their currencies within the range of not more than 1 percent above or below the par value required by the International Monetary Fund. In contrast, U.S. monetary authorities, until March, 1961, maintained the value of the dollar by agreeing to sell gold to foreign official monetary institutions at a fixed price of $35 an ounce. By 1961, however, the U.S. Treasury had become concerned with the volume of short-term funds being transferred for speculation against the dollar's future value and began a program--initially experimental, as Under Secretary Roosa indicated above--of intervention in foreign exchange markets. In February, 1962, the Federal Reserve System began foreign exchange operations on its own account to supplement U.S. Treasury operations.

The fears, expressed through the foreign exchange markets that the U.S. might not maintain the value of the dollar at the level established in 1935 (by maintaining the $35 an ounce price of gold), were abated temporarily by President Kennedy's pledge to maintain the $35 gold price and by the U.S. action program to restore the external balance. It was at this point of temporary quietude in the foreign exchange markets that the Treasury began its intervention. Treasury operations were carried out chiefly in the forward exchange market. A brief explanation of this market will clarify the rationale for the Treasury's choice.

The Forward Exchange Market. General convertibility of the major currencies in 1958 permitted the expansion of international currency dealings that had been curbed by the wartime and postwar disruptions of foreign exchange markets. The removal of the most stringent controls on currency transfers brought the resumption of interest arbitrage and speculation in the future values of convertible currencies. Currencies in foreign exchange markets (for example, the London market) can be purchased and sold for either immediate ("spot") or future ("forward") delivery. The prices of foreign currencies relative to dollars are expressed in terms of a dollar rate of exchange (for example, pound sterling $2.7888, German mark $.25056, and Indian rupee $.13250); and forward rates and spot rates move in response to forces which, although they are similar in the case of both rates, frequently cause the rates to diverge. As the "spread" between the spot and forward rates changes, it affects the movement of short-term funds; a narrow spread tends to attract short-term funds, and a broad spread tends to repel them.

The demand and supply forces that act on the forward market arise principally from commercial import and export covering transactions. An American manufacturer who places an order for electronic equipment with a Netherland firm and agrees to pay $1 million on delivery ninety days hence will wish to avoid the risk that the guilders may cost more in dollars at time of delivery than at the time the order was placed. He will, therefore, cover his risk by buying $1 million guilders forward, i.e., by a "futures contract" that guarantees him the right to obtain $1 million guilders ninety days hence, when delivery is made, at a price agreed upon at the time the order is placed.

While commercial transactions constitute the principal use of forward exchange markets, substantial changes in demand and supply conditions frequently occur as the consequence of (1) investment operations seeking interest arbitrage return and (2) speculation.

Interest arbitrage operations are motivated by the divergence between spot and forward exchange rates. When a short-term investment is purchased, a foreign currency is purchased spot and simultaneously sold forward to mature on the same date as the short-term investment. The yield depends upon the interest rate differential between domestic and foreign short-term investments and also upon the spot-forward spread. In general, given the interest differential, a wider spread discourages an inflow of foreign funds seeking interest arbitrage. Rates of return are figured inclusive of the costs of forward cover.

A typical interest arbitrage decision involves the consideration by an American investor of the purchase of a ninety-day British Treasury bill. Because he wishes to be free to repatriate his funds when the bill matures, the American will want to sell pounds forward in the same amount as the bill. The decision to buy the bill will depend upon the discount on forward pounds, given the interest differential between British and U.S. Treasury bills. If the interest differential is 1.5 percent and the discount on ninety-day forward pounds is 1 cent or .6 percent of the spot rate (pounds bought at $2.780 are sold ninety days hence for $2.770) and the rate per annum is 90/360(.6)=1.5, there is no incentive to invest in British bills rather than U.S. bills. And the greater the cost of cover, the larger must be the interest differential to induce movements of short-term funds for interest arbitrage return.[16]

In contrast to the other forward operations described above, the speculator sells a currency forward without cover expecting to benefit from a decrease in the exchange rate when, at the expiration of his contract, he enters the spot market to acquire the currency to fulfill his contract.

Foreign exchange operations by the U.S. Treasury

and the Federal Reserve System frequently are undertaken to widen the spread between spot and forward dollars in foreign exchange markets. This increases the costs of cover for movements out of dollars. Another objective of foreign exchange operations (which are conducted in spot markets as well as forward markets) is to limit the discounts by which the dollar was sometimes quoted before intervention began. When dollars were heavily discounted, foreign official monetary authorities purchased them to prevent the dollar-domestic currency rate from falling below the limit agreed upon with the International Monetary Fund. Then, as dollars accumulated in foreign official reserves, they were exchanged for gold--causing a reduction in the U.S. supply.

The Role of Foreign Exchange Intervention in U.S. Balance of Payments Policy. Treasury and Federal Reserve System intervention in foreign exchange markets must be appreciated as an ingenious operation to minimize the fluctuations in the dollar's exchange value while other balance of payments policies operated on the basic deficit. Foreign exchange operations do not have any direct effect on the basic deficit. In times of crises, however, these operations have been valuable defenses against excessive dollar depreciation. The Cuban missile crisis and the assassination of President Kennedy are examples of crises in which the dollar was prevented from depreciating by gross amounts through foreign exchange operations and foreign central bank cooperation.

The extent of intercentral bank cooperation since 1962 has been surprising, considering the usual nationalist orientation of central banks. During its first year of foreign exchange operations for its own account, the Federal Reserve System entered into swap agreements (whereby equivalent currency claims on, and liabilities to, another central bank can be created by mutual agreement) totaling $900 million with nine central banks and the Bank for International Settlements. Since 1962 the Federal Reserve foreign currency arrangements have grown to $2.8 billion (1965) and involve eleven countries and the Bank for International Settlements. In addition the Federal Reserve System has overseen the placing with foreign monetary authorities of $1.2 billion of U.S. Treasury foreign currency bonds.

CAPITAL OUTFLOWS

The pivotal role of capital flows in the U.S. external balance was demonstrated by the course of the balance of payments accounts from 1960-63. Table 11 extends the payments and reserves data of Table 9 through 1963 and compares the averages of 1958-60 and 1961-63 entries. Line 7 indicates the average balance on a liquidity basis improved by $1.3 billion between the earlier and later periods and (line 6) shows that average annual reserve asset losses were reduced by nearly $1.0 billion. These improvements were the direct result of a gain in the average balance on goods and services of more than $3.0 billion. The goods and services balance improved so markedly that the liquidity balance might have been expected to reflect the gain to a greater extent than it did, but the avenues down which the gain was in large measure dispersed are clear from lines 3, 4, and 5 in Table 11. U.S. capital outflows, recorded and unrecorded,[17] increased from an average of $1,568 million, 1958-60, to $3,706 million, 1961-63, a drain of nearly $2.2 billion from the $3.0 billion increase on the goods and services balance between the two periods. Unilateral transfers, excluding military transfers (a large portion of which are offset by exports), increased from an average $2,390 million, 1958-60, to $2,682, 1961-63, a negligible drain on the goods and services surplus.

The chagrin felt by the Kennedy Administration over the dissipation of gains in the basic balance through capital outflows foreordained that U.S. balance of payments policies would be amended to cope with capital-flow problems. Short-term interest rates in the United States had been increased in a delicate operation which sought at the same time to constrain long-term rates as a precaution against interruption of the two-year-old economic expansion. Since unemployment of the labor force and under-utilization of industrial capacity were still serious problems at the beginning of 1963, some action course other than increased interest rates would have to be determined. The U.S. balance of payments during the first quarter of 1963 revealed a large increase in capital outflow and an unprecedented quarter-to-quarter deterioration in the liquidity balance. It was immediately clear that a policy-mix including some form of control on capital flows would now be necessary and, given the exigency of the deficit, immediately forthcoming.

TABLE 11

U.S. BALANCE OF PAYMENTS AND RESERVE POSITION, 1960-63
(Millions of Dollars)

	Average 1958-60	1961	1962	1963	Average 1961-63
1. Balance on goods and services[1]	2133	5621	5130	5897	5549
2. Balance on goods and services and unilateral grants[1]	-257	3035	2454	3113	2867
3. Balance on private capital	-754	-1709	-1734	-1475	-1639
A. U.S. capital[2]	-3065	-4180	-3425	-4456	-4020
(a) Short-term	-579	-1556	-544	-785	-962
(b) Long-term & direct	-2486	-2624	-2881	-3671	-3059
B. Foreign capital[2]	2311	2471	1691	2981	2381
(a) Short-term	1981	1939	-115	-23	600
(b) Long-term & direct	330	532	1806	3004	1781
4. U.S. Government capital	-810	-926	-1094	-1664	-1228
5. Errors and omissions	-2	-1006	-1159	-352	-839
6. Reserve assets transactions[3]	1823	606	1533	378	839
7. Balance on liquidity transactions[4]	-3705	-2370	-2203	-2670	-2414
8. Balance on official transactions[5]	-	-1347	-2706	-2044	-2032

Source: *Survey of Current Business*, June, 1966. Table 1, pp.24-25, and Table 3, pp.30-31; and, Department of Commerce News Release, August 17, 1966, "U.S. Balance of Payments in Second Quarter 1966."

1. Excludes military grants.
2. (-) Indicates outflow.
3. (-) Indicates increase in reserve assets (gold, convertible currencies, and gold tranche position, IMF).
4. Derived 1 plus U.S. grants and capital (Chapter 4, Table 7) plus (3A(b)-3B(b)) plus 3A(a) plus foreign commercial credits (Chapter 4, Table 7) plus 5.
5. Line 7 *plus* (3B(b)-commercial credits) *plus* foreign holdings of U.S. Government bonds and notes, except official monetary institutions *plus* foreign official short-term capital, except official monetary institutions.

Revision of U.S. Balance of Payments Policy

An aggravation of the U.S. external balance, attributable to a spurt of capital exports, was disclosed by first quarter, 1963, balance of payments reports. The inevitable consequence was a revision of the policy-mix that had been in operation for two years to strengthen the policies relating to capital outflow. Data which show the quarter-to-quarter increase in long-term capital outflow are given in Table 12. The data for the first and second quarters of

TABLE 12

CAPITAL FLOWS IN THE U.S. BALANCE OF PAYMENTS, 1960-63 (Millions of Dollars)

	1960	1961	1962				1963	
			I	II	III	IV	I	II
			Seasonally Adjusted Annual Rates					
1. Private capital:[1]								
A. U.S. capital, long-term	-2544	-2609	-2224	-3340	-2188	-3312	-4052	-4416
B. Foreign capital, long-term	430	466	780	264	-40	80	-36	812
C. U.S. private capital, short-term	-1348	-1541	-1220	4	-656	-156	348	-2492
D. Foreign capital, short-term	-90	177	-92	-204	52	-220	-72	252
2. U.S. Government capital & grants[2]	-2775	-3370	-3628	-3412	-3396	-3644	-3504	-4744
3. Errors and omissions	-683	-905	-108	-148	-1876	-1968	-488	-568
4. Balance on private capital transactions[3]	-3552	-3507	-2756	-3276	-2832	-3608	-3812	-5844
5. Balance on capital transactions including U.S. Govt.[4]	-6327	-6877	-6384	-6688	-6228	-7252	-7316	-10588
6. Balance on liquidity transactions	-3881	-2370	-3296	-1032	-1772	-2712	-4872	-4456
7. Balance on official transactions	-3402	-1347	-1712	-1144	-3740	-4228	-4324	-3484

Source: Survey of Current Business, June, 1966, Table 1, pp.25-26, and Table 3, pp.30-31.

1. Excluding foreign liquid assets in the U.S.
2. Includes small amounts of misc. govt. non-liquid liabilities; excludes military grants.
3. Excludes foreign liquid assets and special government transactions.

1963, when compared with the data for previous years, disclose a substantial deterioration in the U.S. balance. On a liquidity basis, the deficit (line 6) increased by more than $2 billion from fourth quarter, 1962, to first quarter, 1963, and remained at the increased level through the second quarter, 1963. The increased capital outflows (line 4) in the fourth quarter, 1962, continued in the first quarter, 1963, and greatly increased in the second quarter, 1963. Increasing capital outflow and grants by the U.S. Government added to the private capital outflows and resulted in a much increased total capital imbalance (line 5) compared with previous quarters. The liquidity transactions balance describes a continuously increasing build-up of liquid claims against the United States by official monetary agencies through the first quarter, 1963. Clearly, the deterioration of the generally improving U.S. balance (note, for example, the short-term flow, line 1C) was traceable to capital outflow.

The President's Message on Balance of Payments Policies, July 18, 1963

A revision of the U.S. balance of payments policy was requested by President Kennedy in a special message to the Congress, July 18, 1963. In his introductory statement the President cited the reduction in the liquidity balance deficit accomplished by the policy-mix adopted in response to his February 6, 1961, message, identified the short-term liabilities, long-term assets nature of the U.S. foreign investment balance sheet, and acknowledged the extent to which achievements of reduction in the deficit had been due to "special agreements with friendly foreign countries--for debt repayments, advance payments for military equipment, and U.S. borrowing abroad." The message, as expected, singled out the deterioration of the balance on capital account as an offset to the improved commercial and government overseas expenditures balances and cited the need for a new policy-mix. Despite the increased urgency of the balance of payments problem revealed in the first quarter 1963, data, the President affirmed the intention of the United States to act in accord with the principles cited in his 1961 message:[18]

> Although there is urgent need for further effort, I want to make it clear that in solving

> its international payments problem, this nation will continue to adhere to its historic advocacy of freer trade and capital movements and that it will continue to honor its obligation to carry a fair share of the defense and development of the free world. At the same time, we shall continue policies designed to reduce unemployment and stimulate growth here at home--for the well-being of all free peoples is inextricably entwined with the progress achieved by our own people. I want to make it equally clear that this nation will maintain the dollar as good as gold, freely interchangeable with gold at $35 an ounce, the foundationstone of the free world's trade and payments system.

This statement ruled out import restrictions, capital controls, and any restrictions on government overseas spending not justifiable on foreign policy grounds. It also rejected contractionist economic policies in the domestic economy. The pledge to maintain the existing dollar-gold ratio, considered in isolation from the remainder of the message, was ritualistic and expected.[19]

The New Policy-Mix. The shift to a tighter policy that could improve the balance on capital flows was to be accomplished through imposition of an excise tax on purchases of foreign securities by Americans. Corporations and individuals would be liable for the tax, and it would apply to new and outstanding issues whether purchased in the United States or abroad. The rate of tax would be graduated to achieve the desired effect of adding about 1 percent to the borrower's interest cost. Exceptions, exemptions, and exclusions included purchases of securities already held by an American, direct investments in overseas affiliates or subsidiaries, securities maturing in three years or less, commercial bank loans, securities issued by underdeveloped countries, and international organizations of which the U.S. was a member. If passed by the Congress, the tax--named the interest equalization tax--would be imposed retroactive to July 19, 1963.

Other changes in U.S. balance of payments policies proposed by the President involved increased efforts in export expansion, foreign tourism in the United States, reduction of the foreign exchange costs of Federal expenditures abroad, tax reduction for foreign investors to encourage foreign investment in the United States, an arrangement for a $500 million draw on the IMF, and study of international monetary relations precedent to changes in the existing Bretton Woods System machinery. Of these proposals, the IMF draw arrangement was the most dramatic. It was prompted by the build-up of dollars by the IMF to the limit level of 75 percent of the original U.S. currency subscription to the Fund.

The imposition of an encumbering tax on U.S. capital movements was a sharp departure from historic U.S. practice and was a reluctant choice made among disagreeable options. These options were the tax, capital controls (probably an issues committee), and increased long-term interest rate levels. The capital controls were rejected as "contrary to our basic precept of free markets," and the long-term interest rate increase was rejected on the grounds that it would endanger the economic expansion then only twenty-seven months old. Economic analysis of the tax[20]--its welfare effects, the interest-elasticity of investment, the market-limitation effects on the efficiency of the New York capital market, and so forth--weighed scarcely at all in the determination of the administration to seek the tax; an apparent concomitance between increases in interest rates and the untimely end of the business expansions of 1954-57 and 1958-60 constituted a prima facie case for opting the tax.

A strong case against an interest rate increase in 1963 can be made on the grounds that the punishment was out of proportion to the crime; it was not general cost of credit that the U.S. wished to increase, but the cost of credit to developed countries--chiefly in continental Western Europe--which were using the New York capital market as a marginal source of funds to finance their domestic expansions, and their demand for credit was a miniscule part of the total demand for credit in the United States. Underemployment of the U.S. economy in 1963 ruled out any increase in long-term interest rates beyond the increases (about 22 basic points on long-term Treasury bonds) registered from February, 1961, to July, 1963. The interest equalization tax had as its most attractive feature precisely the fact that it permitted the external effect of an interest rate increase without undesired domestic effects--a veritable "have your cake and eat it" proposition.

A choice between a tax on purchase of foreign securities as opposed to capital controls (for example, a capital issues committee) has an element of "rules versus discretion" about it; how is welfare promoted best, by impersonal or personal forces? The tax is an additional cost, not unlike other costs associated with security offerings. Its impact can be made relatively precise by varying the degree of its inclusiveness. In competitive markets, economic theory demonstrates, the interest rate is the most efficient arbiter of capital, implying that an interest rate-plus-tax systematically applied to raise the interest rate one percent would similarly be an efficient arbiter of capital. By contrast, a capital issues committee _must_ circumvent the market direction of capital allocation. The Radcliffe Commission report[21] was highly critical of British experience with issue control citing, among other reasons, the frightening away of marginal issues, the necessity for detailed evidence to substantiate negative decisions, the tendency for "advisory" decisions to be rubber-stamped by the government as fiat, and promotion of traffic in professional dressing-up of issue applications to improve their chances of passing the committee. The case against the capital issues committee approach seems to have been strong.

In the context of the Treasury Department's repeated criticism of the underdeveloped condition of Continental European markets, and the special studies of those capital markets by the Joint Economic Committee, the interest equalization tax can be credited with seeking long-term effects even though the immediate consequence sought was relief of pressure on the U.S. balance of payments. The long-term effect was the stimulation in Continental Europe of government concern with capital market development. The long-term stability of capital market supply and demand would be improved if the French and German governments moved to reduce their direct role in capital supply and adopted measures that would strengthen the role of financial intermediary institutions in their economies.

CAPITAL MARKET COMPARISONS[22]

The balance of payments policies of the United States have, since 1963, been so closely related to capital flows and capital markets that a brief description of the structural differences between the capital markets of Continental Western Europe and the United States will be useful in providing perspective on the capital flows problem. In brief, the assumption underlying the interest equalization tax was that developed countries in Continental Western Europe had embarked upon ambitious growth programs for which domestic sources of funds (capital) were currently inadequate and, lacking development, would become increasingly inadequate in the future. Retarded development of capital markets contributed to high interest rates and high issue costs--high interest rates through excess demand pressure on limited sources and premiums demanded by lenders to compensate for lack of marketability, and high issue costs through failure to realize economies of scale and to develop underwriting and distribution facilities. Neither underwriters nor financial intermediary institutions had played their expected roles to develop capital markets that possessed depth and flexibility. The interest equalization tax would narrow the yield-differential between the U.S. and foreign securities to which it applied; and, by creating uncertainty about free and unencumbered access to the New York market--the residual source of financing for Continental Western European countries--the tax might stimulate capital market development in those countries.

In May, 1962, U.S. Secretary of the Treasury Dillon had pointedly stated the conviction that was developing in the administration with respect to capital flow problems:[23]

> In the field of portfolio investment, I am not interested in the purchase of foreign equities by American investors, a process that is an essential element of free capital movement. What I am concerned with is the increasing use of the various mechanisms of the

> New York capital market by European borrowers to raise funds for their own internal purposes. Today, the plain fact is that underwriting and distributing facilities in the industrialized countries of continental Western Europe, are generally inadequate to meet the foreseeable needs of domestic borrowers--much less those from abroad. That is not a healthy environment for long-term domestic growth. It inevitably means higher borrowing costs and a shortage of funds for firms and industries that lack their own internal sources of capital. And, when combined with controls and restrictions on capital movements lingering on from earlier days, it has the incongruous effect of shunting to the New York market new issues from the surplus countries, even as we in the United States are endeavoring to erase deficit.
>
> And as long as continental Western Europe continues to operate with inadequate and outmoded capital markets, it can have no solid assurance that the capital required to ensure steady and rapid growth will, in fact, be available.

The Economic Background of Western European Capital Markets

Western Europe's economic growth during the decade of the 1950's averaged 5.7 percent per year in real gross national product. Productivity increases--the average output (GNP) per person employed--achieved annual compound rates during this period of 5.3 percent in West Germany, 4.7 percent in Italy, 4.3 percent in France, and 3.6 percent in the Netherlands.[24] The U.S. rate was 2.1 percent. Table 13 shows the savings rates of Western European countries in relation to GNP. Substantial differences in saving rates are shown. Gross total saving and government saving were higher in each Continental European country shown than in the United States. A higher rate of household saving is shown for West Germany than the United States. It might be expected from the data of Table 13 that public policy in the countries with high government (and government-plus-enterprise) savings encouraged saving

TABLE 13

GROSS SAVING IN WESTERN EUROPEAN COUNTRIES, ANNUAL AVERAGE, 1950-59

(Percent of Gross National Product)

Country	Gross Domestic Saving			Gross Total Saving[2]
	Government	Enterprise[1]	Household	
West Germany	7.7	10.5	8.1	23.2
Italy[3]	2.3	---19.1---		20.8
France	3.9	11.1	3.4	18.6
United Kingdom	2.2	11.4	1.6	14.7
United States	2.5	10.8	5.3	18.0

Source: United Nations, World Economic Survey, 1960, pp.15-56.
1. This category includes public as well as private corporations and, in some countries, household depreciation.
2. Includes gross foreign saving (-)3.1 West Germany, 1.3 Italy, 0.2 France, (-)0.5 United Kingdom.
3. Gross Domestic Saving divisions are for 1955-59 only; hence, the components do not sum to Gross Total Saving, which is the 1950-59 average.

in these sectors. Table 14 shows the level and uses of corporate net income for the countries in Table 13 (except Italy). The data in this table permit some inferences

TABLE 14

LEVEL AND USES OF CORPORATE NET INCOME, ANNUAL AVERAGE, 1950-57

Country	Percent of GNP	Corporate Net Saving[1]		Dividends
		% of Corp. Income Before Taxes	% of Corp. Income After Taxes	% of Corp. Income After Taxes
West Germany	1.8	31.0	68.1	31.9
France	4.3	31.4	47.9	52.1
United Kingdom	5.0	33.4	54.6	45.4
United States	1.9	20.8	41.2	58.8

Source: United Nations, World Economic Survey, 1960, pp.15-56.
1. Depreciation and retained earnings.

about public policy with respect to corporate enterprise saving. The Western European countries apparently pursue policies that permit a higher proportion of corporate saving, before and after taxes, relative to GNP than does the United States. Moreover, the U.S. dividend pay-out rate is substantially higher than the other countries. One form of accommodation to underdeveloped external (market) sources of capital is for public policy to promote corporate internal financing through corporate savings.

An indication of the relative importance of external sources of investable funds is the volume of new security issues relative to fixed capital formation. Table 15 provides this information. The data clearly

TABLE 15

NET NEW SECURITY ISSUES RELATED TO CAPITAL FORMATION, WESTERN EUROPEAN COUNTRIES, 1962

(Millions of Dollars)

	France	West Germany	United Kingdom	United States
Net new issues	2,005	2,957	3,256	23,111
Shares	806	549	717	2,212
Bonds	1,198	2,408	2,540	20,899
Gross fixed capital formation	12,005	21,400	12,953	73,360
Net new issues as percentage of gross fixed capital formation	16.7	13.8	25.1	31.5
Number of securities quoted	2,800[1]	1,825[2]	9,134[3]	7,659[4]

Source: Bank of England, Quarterly Bulletin, July, 1963, p.110.
1. Paris Exchange only.
2. Frankfort Exchange only.
3. London Exchange only.
4. New York Stock Exchange only. Stocks only.

reveal the lesser importance of the German and French new issues markets, relative to the United States and the United Kingdom, as a source of funds for capital formation. Despite the existence of direct placements of loans, securities transactions outside the exchanges, and other deficiencies of the data in Table 15, the conclusion that Continental European markets were underdeveloped in 1962 seems unassailable.

Rates and Costs

The rates prevailing in Western European money and capital markets during the period that began increased foreign borrowing in the New York market reflect the pressure of sustained demand for funds as well as inadequate depth and flexibility. Productivity of capital, given the shortages of labor and capital that existed, was undoubtedly very high relative to the U.S. Table 16 shows the rates on three-month government bills and long-term government bonds in Western Europe and the United States in January of 1963. A pattern of

TABLE 16

INTEREST RATES, WESTERN EUROPE AND THE UNITED STATES, RANGE JULY, 1962, TO JANUARY, 1963
(Percent per Year)

Country	Short-Term	Government Bonds, Long-Term	Central Bank Discount Rate
West Germany	3.01-2.60[1]	6.00-6.10[2]	3.00
France	3.66-3.39[1]	5.10-4.87[2]	4.00
United Kingdom	3.90-3.51[3]	5.98-5.67[2]	4.00
United States	2.94-2.91[3]	4.02-3.88[4]	3.50

Source: United Nations, Monthly Bulletin of Statistics, December, 1964, pp.186-88.
1. Call money rate.
2. Yield in perpetuity.
3. Treasury bill rate.
4. Yield to maturity.

rates is shown that is generally higher, both short-term and long-term, in Western Europe than the United States. The short-term rates in West Germany and France understate the rates comparable to U.K. and U.S. Treasury bills by about .5 because the former are based on call-money rates. Considering the relatively narrow differential between U.S. and Western European central bank discount rates, the market rates (if raised .5 to achieve comparability) imply much higher borrowing costs--especially long-term--in the Continental European markets.

A considerable part of borrowing costs is not revealed by the rates in Table 16; the part excluded consists of underwriting costs, initial taxes, and other taxes on issues, a large proportion of borrowing expense.

TABLE 17

INITIAL COSTS OF PUBLIC ISSUES, WESTERN EUROPE AND U.S., 1963
(Percentages of Sum Raised, Except Where Indicated)

	Domestic Companies Approximate Total Costs		Foreign Govt's. Approximate Total Costs
	Loan	Share	
Belgium	3.5-5	5.3-6.3	na
France	6[1]	7.5-8[2]	na
West Germany	7-8	8-8.5	7-8
Italy	5.5-8.5	na[2]	na
Netherlands	3.3	5.3-5.6	4-5
Switzerland	3-3.5p.v.[3]	4.5[4]	3.5-5
United Kingdom	3	3.3	4.3-4.5
United States	1-2	4-4.5[5]	1.3-4.8

Source: Bank of England, Quarterly Bulletin, III, June 1963, p.115.

1. Including turnover tax.
2. Share issues (apart from rights issues) are infrequent and are usually privately subscribed.
3. p.v. is on par value.
4. This can vary very widely.
5. Ignoring a small fee payable to the Securities and Exchange Commission when the documents are filed.

Table 17 shows these costs for various Western European countries and the United States. The table shows a differential of from 3.5 to 4.0 percentage points in domestic company issue costs between the United States and West Germany and France and a differential of from 3.25 to 5.75 between the United States and Germany in foreign issue costs.[25] A comparison with France cannot be made for 1963 because no foreign issue (except franc-area issues) had been made in France during the previous twelve years.

The capital markets data assembled above provide sufficient evidence that continental markets were costly by U.K. and U.S. standards. It remains to explore the consequences of deficiencies in depth and flexibility on the capacity of these markets to finance investment at the levels planned by Continental European governments.

The Anatomy of Continental European Capital Markets

The markets of greatest interest in this analysis are those in West Germany and France as they appeared in early 1963. Other markets of considerable importance exist in Continental Europe, notably in Amsterdam, Zurich, and Milan. The number of securities quoted on the Amsterdam Stock Exchange, for example, equaled the Paris Exchange and exceeded the Frankfurt Exchange in 1962. Funds from various European countries are channeled to the Amsterdam and Zurich capital markets, which have a long tradition of international lending, but under strict regulation since the war.

The requirements of the West German economy for investment funds are based on annual investment growth of 6 to 7 percent in equipment and 8 to 9 percent in residential and public construction.[26] Production cost increases and a continuous labor shortage are responsible for these needs. In France an ambitious planning experiment envisages annual investment growth of 7 percent, a large increase over the 5.6 percent average level during 1956-61.[27] To finance levels of investment growth at these levels would severely strain domestic capital sources and, out of concern for deficiencies in capital funds, the French Government appointed a committee to study the country's sources of capital market supply. The committee, known as the

Lorain Committee, reported in May, 1963,[28] and recommended many reforms to increase the proportion of savings brought to the capital market in order to meet the needs of the Fourth Plan (1962-65).

In West Germany and France the problems of capital market supply were the same; high levels of saving coexisted with low levels of savings institution assets and nonliquid securities acquisition. Each country approached its problem in a different way. West Germany encouraged corporate internal savings through tax and depreciation policy. France sought funds through government borrowing, then sluiced them to investment uses through the machinery of the national plan.[29] Both approaches inhibit capital market development.

The West German capital markets viewed in 1963 had been unable to renew their traditional prewar role in financing investment. In some degree this is the consequence of the preeminent strength of the large commercial banks,[30] although the government's role in the capital markets has probably had an adverse effect also. Insurance companies were not large net purchases of securities. Gross security issues in 1962 were only 4 percent of GNP, less than half the prewar level.[31] Fixed interest securities in circulation were 18 percent of GNP, compared with 55 percent in the United States.[32] Few issues of securities in circulation in 1962 were issued prior to the 1948 currency reform. From 1950 to 1962, however, the volume of securities increased fiftyfold and doubled between 1958 and 1962. Trading on the stock exchanges had not reached levels that permitted confidence in the marketability of securities among investors, however; and daily volume of known stocks on the exchanges frequently was only a few hundred shares.

The French capital market is entwined with government and paragovernment institutions that have proliferated with the Third and Fourth Plans. M. Delcourt placed the proportion of direct investment by the French Government at 30 percent, and the proportion indirectly financed by the government is probably equal to that figure.[33] Through the operation of credit organizations such as the Caisse des Depôts et Consignations, the Credít National, and the Caisse des Marches de l'Etat, banks discount paper which enables them to make medium-term (five-year) loans.[34] The government is almost exclusively the arbiter of the uses to which the vast resources of the Caisse des Depôts ($45 billion francs in 1962) are put. Directly, the government is a supplier of medium-and long-term capital through the Fonds de Developpement Economique et Social. In 1962 gross investment in France was 61 billion francs of which more than 14 billion (24 percent) was financed directly from public funds; of this amount nearly 3 billion francs (20 percent) was channeled through the FDES accounts--chiefly to nationalized enterprises. Private capital markets tend to the thin and inflexible due to the weight of government operations.

This brief description of West German and French capital markets will suffice to indicate the underdeveloped condition of markets in both countries. The chief consequences of this situation, in 1963, from the U.S. interest, were attraction of U.S. capital, in part because of high interest rates in Europe. Table 18 shows the extent of private long-term capital flows,

TABLE 18

U.S. PRIVATE LONG-TERM INVESTMENT
IN FOREIGN ISSUES, 1962-63
(Millions of Dollars)

	1962	1963		
		I	II	III
By Type:	(Seas. Adj. Ann. Rates)			
Long-term capital	2,495	4,016	3,604	1,928
Purchases, foreign issues	1,131	2,092	2,200	648
New issues	1,076	1,900	1,944	852
Outstanding issues, net	55	192	256	(-)204
Other	1,364	1,924	1,404	1,280
By country of purchase:	(Unadjusted Annual Rates)			
Purchases, foreign issues	1,131	2,216	2,328	512
Western Europe	195	336	776	68
Japan	124	188	320	228
Canada	379	1,328	1,044	204
Other	433	364	188	12

Source: Survey of Current Business, September, 1964, Table 1, p.9, Table 3, pp.12-13.

net, in the U.S. balance of payments and the countries whose securities were purchased. The table shows that the 1962 rate of foreign securities purchases almost doubled by the second quarter, 1963. "Other" investment is largely direct investment. A very large proportion of the new security issues in the first and second quarter, 1963, were Canadian issues. The rate of increase in European issues from 1962 through the second quarter, 1963, however, and the developed and external-surplus condition of Continental European countries justified the concern of the administration over a threatening trend.

The Administration Program in Operation

The President's message of July 18, 1963, on the U.S. balance of payments program had the immediate effect, because of retroactive imposition of the tax, of diminishing U.S. capital outflow to less than half its second quarter level in the third quarter, 1963. Table 19 shows these data. Other capital outflow declined to less than one-fifth of the second quarter level in the third quarter, 1963. New foreign security issues dropped throughout 1963 and held below the second quarter, 1963, level until the fourth quarter, 1964, when Canadian issues (exempt from the tax by Executive Order) bulked unexpectedly large. The Congress passed the interest equalization tax in September, 1964, ending the uncertainty about possible changes in the President's recommendations for its imposition; and an increased level of new foreign issues commenced.

It became apparent at an early date that the exempt areas of private investment--short-term commercial bank loans and direct investment--would in some degree cancel the effects of the interest equalization tax on portfolio investment. Total private capital outflow moved upward from the third quarter, 1963, despite the tax. The transactions category "other" in Table 19, when separated into its components, shows clearly the converse movements of loans by banks and other financial institutions while the portfolio movements were declining. Table 20 shows that a substantial increase in both short-term and long-term lending by banks to foreigners followed the proposal of the interest

TABLE 19

U.S. PRIVATE CAPITAL MOVEMENTS, PAYMENTS, 1963-66
(Millions of Dollars)

	1963				1964				1965				1966
	I	II	III	IV	I	II	III	IV	I	II	III	IV	I
					(Seasonally Adjusted)								
U.S. private capital	1131	1549	670	1106	1360	1385	1589	2189	1605	346	827	912	888
New foreign securities sold in U.S.	485	435	241	89	130	201	147	585	306	244	380	276	459
Direct investment	640	454	304	578	479	536	622	779	1212	859	569	731	630
Other[1]	6	660	125	439	751	648	820	825	87	-757	-122	-95	-201

Source: Survey of Current Business, June, 1966, Table 2, pp.28-29.
1. Includes outstanding securities, redemptions, and bank loans. (-) indicates inflow.

TABLE 20

U.S. PRIVATE CAPITAL MOVEMENTS, PAYMENTS OTHER THAN DIRECT AND NEW FOREIGN SECURITIES ISSUED IN THE U.S., 1963-66

(Millions of Dollars)

Transaction	1963				1964				1965				1966
	I	II	III	IV	I	II	III	IV	I	II	III	IV	I
					(Seasonally Adjusted)								
Other capital movements	6	660	125	339	75	623	820	825	27	-757	-122	-125	-201
Long-term	37	144	132	278	284	157	528	315	462	-163	78	-55	-81
Reported by banks	-10	194	134	436	258	99	257	327	468	-169	58	-126	-123
Reported by other lenders	47	-50	-2	-158	26	58	271	-12	-6	6	20	71	42
Short-term	-67	494	60	298	615	569	365	597	-271	-412	-105	27	14
Reported by banks	-84	447	129	289	402	569	124	428	-21	-144	-51	-104	-137
Reported by other lenders	17	47	-69	9	213	0	241	169	-250	-268	-54	136	151
Other transactions in foreign securities	79	72	15	87	94	40	35	24	49	130	53	-6	21
Redemptions	-43	-50	-52	-50	-54	-38	-38	-63	-55	-52	-42	-73	-113

Source: Survey of Current Business, June, 1966, Table 1, pp.26-27.
(-) Indicates inflow.

equalization tax in the third quarter, 1963. Foreign lending by other lenders, while erratic, tended to move against portfolio investment trends.

As the effects of bank and nonbank financial institution exclusion from the interest equalization tax became apparent, a change in policy was made by President Johnson in February, 1965. By Executive Order the interest equalization tax was extended to apply to commercial banks;[35] and the Congress was requested to extend the tax, originally scheduled to expire at the end of 1965, to 1967. Supplementing these moves, the President initiated, through the Federal Reserve Board, a program of voluntary curbs by banks and nonbank financial institutions to cut back their operations with the banks' goal to limit expansion of claims on foreigners to 5 percent of their outstanding foreign credits as of year-end 1964. Nonbank financial institutions were requested to comply with a related program to decrease their foreign credits and investments. In the Department of Commerce a program was mounted involving the largest nonfinancial corporations to achieve a reduction in the capital outflows induced by their foreign operations. They were asked "to make a maximum effort to expand the net balance of (a) their exports of goods and services plus (b) their repatriation of earnings from the develope countries less (c) their capital outflows to such countries."[36]

The balance of payments results of these new policy actions were generally successful in 1965. Some lag was expected in achieving reductions of capital outflow because the cooperating corporations were not asked to postpone programs already planned. Table 20 shows that "other capital movements" outflow declined and recorded a substantial inflow in each quarter beginning in 1965. Direct investment (Table 19) responded slowly, reaching its highest levels in the first two quarters of 1965, but declined in succeeding quarters. The record high levels of direct investment made it necessary to look to these outflows for further improvement of the deficit Consequently, new guidelines were developed for nonfinancial corporations requesting that combined 1965 and 1966 direct investment outflows (plus earnings retained abroad) in specified developed countries and mineral exporting nations be held to no more than 90 percent of the total of these items in the years 1962-64. The joint year target was set for the years 1965 and 1966 in order not to penalize firms which had cut back in 1965 and in order to seek greater restraint by those which had invested more heavily in 1965.[37] Financial institution guidelines for 1966 permitted about the same outflow as in 1965, but nonbank financial institutions received more detailed guidelines than previously.

Anticipations for improved external balance in 1966 were not optimistic because of the defense expenditures occasioned by the Vietnam War--a balance of payments drain that might run between $500 million and $1 billion.

EMERGENCE OF A POLICY-MIX

As a consequence of gradual improvement in the U.S. external balance following the adoption (and subsequent extension) of policy recommendations made by President Kennedy in mid-1963, a mixture of actions--including measures to encourage exports, to discourage capital outflow, to induce surplus countries to reduce their surpluses, and to promote changes in the international monetary system--came to be recognized at home and abroad as the U.S. balance of payments policy. The measures adopted, and the weight given to one measure as compared with another, were not accepted by all parties in interest to the U.S. external position;[38] but the degree of concensus that existed by mid-1965 was such that the policy-mix could be expected to stand. That the balance of payments measures employed had effected a decrease in the U.S. deficit is indicated by the data in Table 21. The 1963 liquidity transactions deficit was almost halved by 1965, due in part to increased exports. A somewhat larger decrease occurred in the official transactions deficit. Preliminary data for the first half of 1966 indicate a slight increase in the deficit on liquidity transactions but a large decrease in the official transactions deficit, from $1,302 million in 1965 to $874 million, seasonally adjusted annual rate.

TABLE 21

U.S BALANCE OF PAYMENTS AND RESERVE POSITION, 1962-65
(Millions of Dollars)

	1962	1963	1964	1965
1. Balance on goods and services[1]	5130	5897	8490	6957
2. Balance on goods and services and unilateral grants[1]	2454	3113	5725	4163
3. Balance on private capital	-1734	-1475	-3211	-3381
A.U.S. capital[2]	-3425	-4456	6523	-3690
(a)Short-term	-544	-785	-2146	761
(b)Long-term & direct	-2881	-3671	-4377	-4451
B.Foreign capital[2]	1691	2981	3312	309
(a)Short-term	-115	-23	113	146
(b)Long-term & direct	1806	3004	3199	163
4. U.S. Government capital	-1094	-1664	-1674	-1575
5. Errors and omissions	-1159	-352	-1011	-429
6. Reserve assets transactions[3]	1533	378	171	1222
7. Balance on liquidity transactions[4]	-2203	-2670	-2798	-1337
8. Balance on official transactions[5]	-2706	-2044	-1546	-1305

Source: Survey of Current Business, June, 1966. Table 1, pp.24-25, and Table 3, pp.30-31; and, Department of Commerce News Release, August 17, 1966, "U.S. Balance of Payments in Second Quarter 1966."

1. Excludes military grants.
2. (-) Indicates outflow.
3. (-) Indicates increase in reserve assets (gold, convertible currencies, and gold tranche position, IMF).
4. Derived 1 plus U.S. grants and capital (Chapter 4, Table 7) plus (3A(b)-3B(b)) plus 3A(a) plus foreign commercial credits (Chapter 4, Table 7) plus 5.
5. Line 7 plus (3B(b)-commercial credits) plus foreign holdings of U.S. Government bonds and notes, except official monetary institutions plus foreign official short-term capital, except official monetary institutions.

Until such time as the official settlements transaction deficit is eliminated, the U.S. balance of payments policy will continue the mix of measures in operation in mid-1966. Exports will be encouraged, and public policy will attempt to preserve price stability; the interest equalization tax will effectively narrow interest differentials; voluntary controls on capital outflow will limit the capital accounts deficit and encourage borrowing abroad, putting pressure on European capital markets to develop savings sources; and special transactions, such as prepayments of debt and military expenditures, will offset some European dollar receipts. When the deficit on official transactions approaches zero, more basic long-term measures will be sought.

Long-term measures will involve changes in the international monetary mechanism established at Bretton Woods more than twenty years ago. The goals sought in international monetary "reform" will be to (1) relieve the U.S. dollar as a key currency from the currency pressures that have accumulated over the years since Bretton Woods and (2) to arrange for additions to the world's stores of liquidity (official reserves) that will be required in the absence of U.S. deficits, the chief source of reserve additions during the postwar years.

SHORT-TERM TRADE-OFFS AND LONG-TERM EXPECTATIONS

It is generally appreciated in the United States and abroad that the restrictions on capital outflow and the special transactions, such as debt prepayments, are temporary and exceptional measures employed in support of U.S. balance of payments policy only in the short term, pending elimination of the official transactions deficit. One of the reasons for electing voluntary curbs to reduce outflows of capital was that such curbs, in contrast to legislative curbs, can more quickly be removed when the need for them has passed. The onerous nature of curbs of any sort on capital flows--especially in the United States, the only country which has continuously permitted free and unfettered capital transfers--is widely appreciated. There is a limit to the degree of geographic discrimination that can be practiced in a world economy in which capital is highly mobile. Developing countries would suffer, despite exemptions; and some other countries would, unintentionally, suffer. By 1966 the IMF had become sufficiently concerned to urge early removal of the restrictions imposed by the U.S. and the U.K.[39]

> The reduction in aggregate imbalances during 1965 was brought about in part by the U.S. program to restrain the outflow of capital and by similar U.K. measures. The less developed countries have largely been insulated from the effects of these measures, which have, as a side effect, helped to broaden international capital markets outside the two reserve centers, a development that must in itself be welcomed. At the same time, the measures taken by the two reserve centers to reduce the outflow of capital have had some adverse effect on the payments positions of several countries. Many countries have been affected by the increases in interest rates that have taken place in capital markets everywhere. It is difficult to distinguish the effects of these and other causes, but in combination they have made it much more difficult for many countries to attract foreign capital, and have intensified the balance of payments problems of a number of countries dependent on an inflow of private capital to assist their economic growth. While less harmful than measures that would attempt to achieve balance of payments adjustment through deflation, restraints on the international transfer of capital may lead to a misallocation of resources and a reduction in global economic growth. It is to be hoped, therefore, that member countries will find it possible to allow capital to move more freely from country to country by appropriate measures, including the reduction or elimination not only of the restraints recently introduced by the two reserve centers but also those which a number of countries have been practicing over a long period.

The Effects of the U.S. Balance of Payments Policy in Europe

The evidence that U.S. capital outflow restriction has had the desired effect in Europe is the large increases in foreign borrowing, especially in West Germany, and the measures taken throughout Europe to increase savings flows to capital markets. A very large market in dollars and other convertible currency deposits (the Euro-dollar market) had developed in London by the early 1960's and had spread elsewhere. This market provided funds on a short-term basis but were frequently borrowed by banks and lent long-term, producing dangerous liquidity possibilities. In the wake of the U.S. policies on capital outflow restriction, however, especially the voluntary curbs on nonfinancial corporations, a broader, long-term market developed. Public policy, especially in West Germany,[40] was partly responsible for the development of a wider, long-term market by stimulating the mobilization of funds for borrowing.

French and West German tax laws, following U.S. curbs on capital outflows, were amended to stimulate "savings" by lightening taxes on holders of stocks and bonds. In June, 1965, a law was passed in West Germany which required significant changes in the information made available to stockholders by West German corporations. The objective was to induce confidence in share-owning and stimulate accumulation of private securities. For the same reason, the 2.5 percent securities tax was repealed in January, 1965.

European markets have recently experimented with raising capital by sharing a loan among the six Common Market countries. This extends a practice in which a loan to Japan was shared between Zurich and Frankfurt in 1964. The prospects for large-scale, supranational capital pooling must be appraised as doubtful, but the seeds have been planted.

Throughout Europe the impact of the American policies has been to increase competition for long-term funds and foreign exchange. In Germany the interest rate structure has moved upward, and a voluntary quota system has been employed to control access to the capital market. Despite increasing monetary tightness, foreign borrowing has taken place in the German capital market, initially by Scandinavian and Japanese borrowers, but later by borrowers from other countries including the United States. Sufficient evidence already exists to support the view that capital markets of greater depth and flexibility, able to make large foreign loans, have come into operation in Continental Europe. Future development may be either in the direction of a new world capital market in Frankfurt or the development of several markets in different cities, each market having a large capacity and, in all likelihood, specialized financial institutions.[41] In 1965, according to a tally by the Banking Federation of the European Economic Community, reported in the *Journal of Commerce*, January 10, 1966, the volume of international loans placed in Europe reached a total of $1.3 billion. The majority of foreign loans, however, are made to other European countries.

A highly regarded study to project the U.S. external balance for five years was made by the Brookings Institution in 1963 at the request of the Council of Economic Advisers.[42] This study dealt with the *basic* U.S. balance (net exports of goods and services plus long-term capital) and cited the following factors as essential considerations in the projection: "(1) the relationship between rates of growth of real domestic demand and potential output in the United States and Western Europe; (2) changes in the competitive relationship between the United States and Western Europe; and (3) movements of long-term capital, especially between the United States and Europe."[43] These changes in economic growth, prices, and long-term capital movements determined the course of the U.S. external balance. On one set of assumptions--considered optimistic by critics in that a smaller degree of inflation was assumed for the United States than Western Europe--a substantial improvement was projected in the basic balance by 1968.[4] On another set of assumptions--lower rates of growth in the U.S. and Western Europe and less inflation in Europe the projected improvement was much less, $200 million, as compared with $2.7 billion under the first set of assumptions.[45]

It was apparent by 1965 that the improvement of the basic balance was exceeding the average rate derived from the Brookings study projection. Mr. Walter Salant, testifying on this observation before the Senate Committee on Banking and Currency, concluded, "most of the cut in the basic deficit reflects fundamental improvement. Very little of the gain in our competitive position or in our receipts of investment income can be attributed to transitory factors or emergency programs, although some of the 1964 rise in our trade surplus may have resulted from deficits in the non-European world, if they occurred."[46]

The Brookings study warned against making inferences from simple statistical projections of balance of payments data; and the capricious movements of many annual and quarterly series--especially capital flows--as well as the importance of interplay among variables, certainly justify the warning. Some important series yield an excellent fit to nonlinear equations, however; and guarded interpretation of such series can be useful in weighing near-term balance of payments expectations. Exports and imports of goods and services constitute one such series. Table 22 gives 1965 actual annual data and projections for five years hence. The projections show a steady increase in net exports (exports less imports) that bodes well for the major factor underlying the basic balance. Similar equations fitted to quarterly data, first quarter, 1963, to second quarter, 1966, however, disclose a decreasing net export balance, indicating that more recent data may have reversed the long-term favorable trend.[47] Capital movements and income from investments are too variable to yield useful prediction equations and are, in any case, influenced much more than exports and imports by government policy.[48]

Any search for evidence of a trend among existing data that will indicate decisively improvement or deterioration in the U.S. external position must be disappointed. Capital flows, under the restraint of government policies to restrict their net movement, have ceased to contribute to the U.S. deficit in the magnitudes that occurred in 1962-63. What their movement will be in the absence of controls is shrouded in doubt. Increased price inflation in the United States thus far in 1966 threatens adverse change in a major factor underlying the U.S. balance of payments position. Net exports appear to have declined substantially since their 1964 peak. Accordingly, the mix of policies faces strengthening again at a time when the eager hope had been that the agenda of policies might turn to international monetary reform.[49]

TABLE 22

U.S. BALANCE OF INTERNATIONAL PAYMENTS,
PROJECTIONS OF EXPORTS AND IMPORTS, 1965-70

(Billions of Dollars)

	Exports[1]	Imports[2]	Exports(-)Imports
1965(actual)	39.0	32.0	7.0
1965(predicted)	38.0	30.2	7.8
1966	40.5	31.7	8.8
1967	43.2	33.2	10.0
1968	45.9	34.8	11.1
1969	48.8	36.4	12.4
1970	51.8	38.1	13.7

Source: Survey of Current Business, June, 1966, Table 1, pp.24-25.

1. Excludes military exports. Equation: $Exports=15.47+.391X+.064X^2$, $r=.972$, standard error $(S_{y.xx}2)=1.8$.

2. Equation: $Imports= 12.79+.700X+.024X^2$, $r=.983$, standard error $(S_{y.xx}2)=1.1$.

Notes to Chapter 5

1. Excluding U.S.S.R., other Eastern European countries, China Mainland, and North Korea. A substantial proportion of gold was required as a "backing" for Federal Reserve Bank liabilities, chiefly notes. In 1964 the gold certificate requirement for backing deposit liabilities of the Federal Reserve Banks was eliminated, freeing $5 billion of gold for external deficit service.

2. George N. Halm, "Special Problems of a Key Currency in Balance-of-Payments Deficit," in _Factors Affecting the United States Balance of Payments_ (Washington: Joint Committee on the Economic Report, 1962), p.6.

3. Excluding U.S.S.R., other Eastern European countries, China Mainland, and North Korea.

4. Austria, Belgium, France, German Federal Republic, Italy, Netherlands, Spain, Sweden, Switzerland, U.K., Canada.

5. Paul Høst-Madsen, "Gold Outflows from the United States, 1958-63," _IMF Staff Papers_, XI, July, 1964, p.250. Høst-Madsen's formula for U.S. gold outflow, based on the 1958-63 period and the International Monetary Fund concept of the U.S. deficit, is Gold Sales=.60 U.S. deficit-2/3 addition to world gold reserves.

6. Seymour Harris compiled a list of twenty-eight suggestions for "treating the American Balance of Payments," and the list embraces only relatively moderate proposals; some frequently discussed proposals, such as flexible exchange rates, and some bizarre proposals, such as substitution of indirect for direct taxes at the Federal level, are not included. Seymour E. Harris, editor, _The Dollar in Crisis_ (New York: Harcourt Brace, 1961), pp.2-3.

7. Orthodox theory would hold that an expanding economy short of full employment would result in increased imports and decreased exports in the merchandise account and increased capital imports and decreased

capital exports, the net effect on the payments balance determined by supply and demand elasticities.

8. An appraisal of the American literature is attempted for the benefit of European readers by Walter P. Egle, "American Reaction to the Balance of Payments Deficit," 93, No.2, Weltwirtschaftliches Archiv, 1964, pp.273-8

9. The message is reprinted in Harris, op.cit., pp. 295-307.

10. Ibid., p.295.

11. Ibid., p.296.

12. Ibid., p.296.

13. Ibid., p.299.

14. The reference to monthly meetings refers to the so-called Basel Group which meets at the Bank for International Settlements.

15. Robert V. Roosa, "The Beginning of a New Policy," in Emergence of an American Balance of Payments Policy (Washington: Joint Committee on the Economic Report, 1962), pp.328-29.

16. Cf. Normal Crump, The ABC of the Foreign Exchanges (London: Macmillan and Co., Ltd., 1963), p.123.

17. Errors and omissions, line 5, are considered to represent largely unrecorded flows of short-term capital.

18. New York Times, July 19, 1963.

19. Since the occasion of Britain's devaluation in 1949 and Sir Stafford Cripps' disclaimer that his country had no intention to devalue, until the event was a fait accompli, it has been assumed that denial of an intention to devalue is part of the devaluation ritual.

20. The author has elsewhere discussed the difficulties of evaluating the interest equalization tax in terms of economic analysis. John D. Hogan, "A New Tax Tool:

The Interest Equalization Tax," Proceedings of the Fifty-eighth National Tax Conference (Harrisburg: National Tax Association, 1966), pp.563-72.

21. There is no intention in this statement to deny that other deflationary forces were at work.

22. The data presented in this section are the unrevised data as they were available to the Kennedy Administration in 1963. Much of this discussion is drawn from the author's "Western European Capital Markets and U.S. Capital Outflow Restriction," The Quarterly Review of Economics and Business, 4, Summer, 1964, pp.65-78, and "Western European Capital Markets and the Role of Life Insurance Companies," Journal of Risk and Insurance, 31, June, 1964, pp.57-68.

23. Address before the American Bankers Association Annual Monetary Conference, Rome, May, 1962.

24. Twentieth Century Fund, The New Europe and Its Economic Future (New York: Macmillan, 1964), pp.5-6.

25. The differentials shown here are conservative because costs in some capital markets involve compounded stamp duties on transfers, and other costs related to transfers, that cannot be measured.

26. Federal Minister of Economic Affairs, Report on Economic Trends in 1962 and Prospects for 1963 (Bonn: Ministry of Economic Affairs, 1963), p.12.

27. John Hackett, "Planning for Growth: The French Experiment," OECD Observer, June, 1963, p.13.

28. Rapport par le Comité Chargé d'Etudier le Financement des Investissements (Paris: May, 1963).

29. A description of this process, notable for its candor, is given by Jean-Paul Delcourt, "Means by Which the State Can Influence Economic Development Under the Plan," French and Other National Plans (Paris: Comité Europeen et Social, 1963), pp.23-27.

30. Commercial banks in West Germany, as in Switzer-

land, function as investment institutions as well as commerical credit institutions. They act as under-writers of securities, and the largest proportion of securities trading is effected through them. The seventy-five banks represented in the Frankfurt Exchange (the largest of eight in Germany) dominate transactions. Interlocking directorates are common and extend considerably the power of the commercial banks in the West German economy.

31. Deutsche Bundesbank, Monthly Report, October, 1963, pp.101, 126.

32. Ibid., p.103. Federal debt in Germany is negligible If U.S. Federal debt were excluded from the U.S. totals in the comparison, the U.S. ratio would be 32 percent.

33. Jean-Paul Delcourt, op.cit., p.32. Mr. Delcourt indicates the role of paragovernment institutions in financing equipment: "The Crédit National is in France the bank that approves almost all credits for equipment, be it credits for medium or long-term loans. More than 90 percent of bank loans for equipment are at present granted by the Crédit National." (p.25.)

34. Ministere des Finances, Statistiques et Studes Finances, Supplement (Seizieme Rapport Annual de Conseil National du Crédit), August, 1962, p.89.

35. This extension was under authority of the so-called Gore Amendment to the Interest Equalization Tax Act.

36. Council of Economic Advisers, Economic Report of the President; transmitted to the Congress January, 1966 (Washington: Council of Economic Advisers), p.166.

37. Ibid., p.167.

38. The Managing Director of the IMF, for example, in his address to the 1965 IMF Annual Meeting, conspicuously refrained from any discussion of U.S. balance of payments policies announced seven months previously, althoug he discussed British balance of payments policies in detail. International Monetary Fund, Summary Proceedings, Annual Meeting (Washington: IMF, 1965), pp.18-20. Howev

cautious approval of the U.S. actions was registered in the 1965 IMF Annual Report. International Monetary Fund, 1965 Annual Report (Washington: IMF, 1965), pp. 5-6. The 1966 report was critical of the capital outflow restrictions but conceded that they had produced good results in the U.S. and abroad. International Monetary Fund, 1966 Annual Report (Washington: IMF, 1966), p.5.

39. IMF, 1966 Annual Report, op.cit., p.5.

40. An account of current developments in the West German capital market and West German public policy is given in a recent publication by the Economic Research Group of Amsterdam-Rotterdam Bank N.V., Deutsche Bank (AG), Midland Bank, and Societe Generale de Banque: Generale Bank Maatschappis, Capital Markets in Europe (London: ERG, 1966), pp.28-44.

The Group, summarizing the recent developments in European capital markets, credited U.S. capital outflow curbs as a major stimulus: "During the last few years, the development of international arrangements within Europe for the provision of medium and long-term funds has made considerable headway. Progress has been particularly rapid since the introduction of the interest equalization tax in the United States in 1964 reduced the attraction of the New York market to foreign borrowers. The demands on the European markets have been further increased by the efforts of the U.S. Government to limit the outflow of capital and, to a lesser extent, by the U.K. restrictions on direct overseas investment." (p.100.)

41. See, for example, the following evaluations of prospects for European financial integration and development of financial centers: Charles F. Kindleberger, "European Economic Integration and the Development of a Single Financial Center for Long-Term Capital," Weltwirtschaltliches Archiv, 90, 1963, pp.189-208; Jacques Mertens de Wilmars, "Währungs perspectiven des Gemeinsamen Marktes," ibid., pp.350-76; Edgar Salin, "Fur eine europäische Währung," Fundamentale Fragen künftiger Währungspolitik, J.C.B. Mohr and Paul Liebeck, eds. (Tübingen: 1965), pp.199-219;

David Williams, "The Development of Capital Markets in Europe," IMF Staff Papers, XII, March, 1965, pp.37-60; and Heinz Portmann, Ansätze zu einem europäischen Kapital markt (Zürich: Schweizerischen Bankgelsellschaft, 1965).

42. Walter S. Salant, et.al., The United States Balance of Payments in 1968 (Washington: The Brookings Institution,1963).

43. Ibid., p.212.

44. Ibid., p.215.

45. Ibid., p.216.

46. Walter S. Salant, A New Look at the U.S. Balance of Payments (Washington: The Brookings Institution, 1965) p.16.

47. The equation for the quarterly data, fitted to fourteen quarters, first quarter, 1963, through second quarter, 1966, in billions of dollars, seasonally adjusted, are:

$Exports=7.42+.295X-.0056X^2$ $r=.952$; $S_{y.xx}2=.309$
$Imports=6.46+.010X+.013X^2$ $r=.985$; $S_{y.xx}2=.167$

For the third quarter, 1966, through fourth quarter, 1967, the projections are:

Exports	Imports	Exports(-)Imports
10.59	9.58	1.01
10.71	10.00	.71
10.83	10.45	.38
10.92	10.92	.00
11.02	11.42	-.40
11.09	11.9	-.81

48. The equations for capital movements are given below with their standard errors, indicating the poor fit obtained. (Data: first quarter, 1963, through second quarter, 1966, seasonally adjusted, millions of dollars.)

1. U.S. $capital=-917.56-154.43X+12.51X^2$
   $r=.489$ $S_{y.xx}2=452.82$
2. Foreign $capital=1128.03-129.76X+5.04X^2$
   $r=.414, S_{y.xx}2=569.68$.

3. Net capital, U.S. and foreign=198.93-280.66X+17.35X^2 r=.737,$S_{y.xx}2$=272.35.
4. Net income on investment, annual data, 1950-65, is given by the following: net investment income (millions of dollars)=959.63+48.21X+3.96X^2 r=.965 $S_{y.xx}2$=161.86.

49. In an address to the IMF-IBRD meeting, August 28, 1966, Secretary of the Treasury Fowler hinted that, unless surplus countries became more cooperative, the U.S. might take drastic action.

CHAPTER 6 CAPITAL FLOWS AND EXTERNAL ADJUSTMENT

Preceding chapters have reviewed the interwar and wartime background of the Bretton Woods system, outlined the resurgence of Europe in the world economy, and described the transition from dollar scarcity to dollar redundancy resulting in U.S. efforts to meet its key currency obligations by framing policies consistent with the Bretton Woods Agreement. The persistency of the U.S. external deficit, and the difficulties posed for the U.S. in dealing with it under the Bretton Woods system, whether or not the deficit is eliminated, have forced the U.S. to seek basic changes in the prevailing international monetary system. If the deficit is eliminated in the near future, the U.S. voice will be strengthened in international monetary affairs and in leadership of the movement for monetary reform. A protracted continuation of the deficit despite the comprehensive U.S. program to curb capital outflow, and despite the U.S. record of price stability, underemployment, and (during the past year) high interest rates, will certainly bring stronger antideficit policies, probably including retaliation against surplus countries which pursue reserve-hoarding policies. Either way the international monetary system will ultimately be changed.

Capital flows will be conceded a pivotal role when the blueprints for international monetary reform are prepared--because the reformed system is almost certainly going to be one based on fixed exchange rates or, allowing for the possibility of some widening in permissible departures from par values, near-fixed exchange rates. Given fixed rates, the universal goal of full employment without inflation, and generally free movement of goods, the chief equilibrating factor in the short and intermediate term must be capital flows.

Despite the close cooperation of world monetary authorities, who have rescued the pound each year since 1964, and the support of prescriptions for increased capital mobility (e.g., the OECD Code for Liberalization of Capital Movements), the odds against successful construction of a system based on equilibrating capital flows must be considered high. The odds are, no doubt, improved compared to the stark evaluation made by Myrdal a decade ago:[1]

> Among the heavy odds against the restoration of a reliable international payments system is the decline of the international capital market...I think it no exaggeration to say that no economist of the earlier generation would have given any chance whatsoever to an international payments system--without discriminatory interferences in trade--under presently prevailing and foreseeable conditions for long-term capital movements.

BALANCE OF PAYMENTS ADJUSTMENTS UNDER BRETTON WOODS

The operation of adjustment mechanisms which, following some disturbance such as a capital outflow, restore equilibrium to a country's monetary relations with other countries may, in a gold coin standard world, have approximated the automatic sequence usually depicted in introductory textbooks. Some doubts were raised in Chapter 2 about inexorable operation of the gold standard system. There can be no question, however, about the judgment that, in a world of relative price rigidities and national full employment commitments, the operation of the tendencies toward automatic correction of external disequilibria--however powerful they may have been in the golden days of the gold standard--has been enfeebled and slowed. It is clear, too, that in the degree to which the equilibrium-inducing forces have been curbed, the occurrence of disequilibrium has become a more threatening predicament to the country out of balance; the policy options that may be employed are few and their leverage on the basic problem more limited, making improvement slow and frustrating. With the increased mobility of capital, any protraction of a country's external imbalance invites reserve loss, and, as a result, reduction of confidence in the country's currency. Thus, the country in disequilibrium faces distasteful prospects that may lead other countries to accumulate large stocks of reserve assets and safeguard them by restrictions on capital flows.

Adjustments for disequilibria were provided, it was assumed, at Bretton Woods. Exchange rates were to be pegged--to make them a stabilizing force--but they could be adjusted by any country as required (up to 10 percent) to correct fundamental disequilibrium. For temporary disequilibrium, they could vary plus or minus 0.5 percent from the established par value (plus or minus 2 percent over-all, de facto, since most countries stabilized to the dollar as a base).[2] The basic forces in the economy--price and income changes--would then provide the adjustment mechanism which operated to correct disturbances in the international monetary relations among countries. To cushion adjustment strains, countries could borrow foreign exchange from the Fund.

Fixed Exchange Rates Versus Variable Exchange Rates

The Bretton Woods conferees sought a substitute for the ideal gold standard system, but without its rigidities. It was reasoned that the volume and stability of world trade would be larger under fixed exchange rates than under variable rates, a desirable feature if the adjustment process could be given more flexibility in operation than the gold standard had provided. Adjustment under the Bretton Woods system, therefore, was to be shared between the internal economy (prices and economic growth) and the external economy (exchange rates and capital controls). Presumably, equilibrium, internal and external, could be jointly achieved rather than achieved one at the expense of the other.

The history of international monetary relations since 1947, contrary to the Bretton Woods assumptions, witnessed frequent exchange rate changes in the first few years, then infrequent changes until 1958, and virtually no changes among major trading countries since then.[3] Thus, the flexible peg, in operation, has become a fixed peg, no change having occurred since 1958 and no concentration of changes since 1949. In effect, the burden of adjustment has been thrown onto domestic prices and incomes, factors which have themselves become inflexible.

After 1958 and the achievement of convertibility, central banks began intervening directly in the exchange markets to defend the external values of their currencies, and monetary reserves (liquidity)[4] became a major factor in international monetary relations. Some officials began to raise questions about the growth of the monetary reserves necessary to defend currencies in the international exchange markets and the distribution of these reserves. With prices and incomes becoming more inflexible, and exchange rates fixed de facto, what adjustments were possible in the absence of import and capital restrictions? One answer, recovered scarred from past service in international monetary affairs, was to throw the adjustment onto the exchange rate; that is, make exchange rates flexible day-to-day and hour-to-hour.[5]

The case for flexible exchange rates benefits from the impeccable logic of its construction and the disarming beauty of its fit in a world ridden by price, income, and exchange rate rigidities. If governments are committed to stability, full employment, and growth, and fixed exchange rates pose the danger of liquidity deficiencies in the long run, the factor that must "give" is the exchange rate. Rather than be fixed (even within a range), the rate should be surrendered to the market place--the exchange market--where the dynamics of import and export net balances would (with beneficial assistance from speculators) establish a country's exchange rate, and also change it as required, in direct relationship to the external net balance. Export surpluses would induce high (export-penalizing) rates and import surpluses would induce low (export-assisting) rates. Moreover, the need for foreign exchange (liquidity) balances would disappear. That the balance of sentiment among international monetary experts should be heavily weighted against this proposal, which might have been designed as an answer to the U.S. payments problem, indicates that it promises more benefits than it is apt to deliver.

The case against a flexible exchange rate system is composed in part of the difficulties involved in the transition to a new system, in part of poor experience with the system by countries that have tried it, and in part of the numerous risks that must be assumed in trusting that speculation in foreign exchange would be stabilizing rather than destabilizing, and that uncertainty about the future pattern of rates would not disrupt trade and reduce international investment. It is possible that, in the absence of the close cooperation among countries required to make the Bretton Woods system work, and given sufficiently onerous adjustment problems, the risks might be justified. Neither of these limit situations has yet been encountered by the United States.

Experience during the eight years that have elapsed since the achievement of external convertibility by major currencies indicates that international trade and national economic growth can be achieved within the Bretton Woods system. World exports have increased in real terms by 66 percent and world industrial production has increased by 55 percent. Experience also indicates the vulnerability of the Bretton Woods system and its basic dependence upon cooperation among nations. In 1964 the U.S., the IMF, and several European countries were required to shore-up two major currencies that came under speculative attack--the British pound and the Italian lira. The fact that crises which develop could call for summary support action is itself a reflection on the system; but the necessary support was forthcoming and ad hoc rescue operations have become less necessary with the negotiation of General Agreements to Borrow by the Group of Ten,[5] supplementing IMF resources. One dimension of the cooperation assumed necessary in forming the Bretton Woods system has not come to pass: The burdens on surplus-position countries to eliminate their surpluses have not matched the weight of the burdens on deficit-position countries to eliminate their deficits. This point will be taken up again in a later section.

CAPITAL NEEDS AND CAPITAL SUPPLY

Capital requirements and the capacity of capital markets to supply them were discussed in Chapter 5 with reference to Continental Europe. This section raises another problem, the sufficiency of capital in a global perspective to meet the needs of developing countries. For many reasons--humanitarian and self-interest--this aspect of the capital flows problem has importance, especially in connection with the U.S. balance of payments program. Despite efforts to insulate the developing countries from the effects of U.S. capital outflow restrictions, the flow of funds from the United States to these countries is certainly being affected.

The evidence that capital movements to less-developed countries have failed to reach the magnitudes required by these countries and, by this failure, have contributed to international economic instability, is impressive. In calling for a program to increase the flow of capital to less-developed countries, the Secretary General of the United Nations made the following appraisal of the capital flows problem that prevailed in the late 1950's:[6]

> As regards long-term capital flows and assistance, the total net flow to low-income countries increased considerably during the later part of the decade (more rapidly than the national incomes of the wealthier countries or of the receiving countries), but remained considerably less than 1 per cent of the combined national incomes of the wealthier countries. In spite of some progress, much of it was still made available on a basis offering no real assurance of its continuity to individual countries; it remained split up amongst a multiplicity of sources, forms and purposes; the share of multilateral aid through the United Nations system remained small. There was no clear evidence that a satisfactory basis had been found for a sustained, assured and more widely distributed flow of private capital to developing countries, nor indeed was it certain that such a flow could be expected until development had gathered more momentum. In any case, the mounting pressure of commitments for repayment of principal and interest or profits on previous investments, combined with the uncertainty and lack of dynamism of export earnings in many under-developed countries, underscored the importance of increasing the proportion of assistance in forms that would bear less heavily on the balance of payments than

> conventional loans. Furthermore, the fall in commodity prices in recent years has nullified much of the net increase in the assistance given to the developing countries.

An increasing part of funds supplied to underdeveloped countries was being siphoned off for service of previously incurred debts and the net amounts of funds available for employment in development was to that extent diminished. Table 23 shows the percentage of guaranteed debt repayable over the next five years for

TABLE 23

GUARANTEED DEBT REPAYABLE OVER NEXT FIVE YEARS
(Percentage of Public and Publicly Guaranteed Debt)

50% or More	40-49%	30-39%	20-29%
Argentina	Burma	Ecuador	Bolivia
Brazil	Ceylon	Ethiopia	Dominican Republic
Guatemala	Chile	Iran	India
Israel	Colombia	Nicaragua	Pakistan
Mexico	Costa Rica	Nigeria	Paraguay
Philippines	El Salvador	Peru	Sudan
Turkey	Spain	Thailand	Uruguay
Venezuela			
Yugoslavia			

Source: Organisation for Economic Cooperation and Development, The Flow of Financial Resources to Less-Developed Countries (Paris: OECD, 1964), p.86.

selected less-developed countries. Those countries at the upper end of the spectrum with respect to debt burden face not only a greatly diminished level of net usable funds out of their gross receipts of funds, but also a growing reluctance on the part of lenders to continue the same rate of capital flow--because of an implied decrease in ability to service loans. The annual increase in public and publicly guaranteed debt of the less-developed countries averaged about

15 percent during the period 1955-62, and some of these countries (Argentina, India, and Pakistan) averaged considerably higher.[7] Total net flow of receipts of the less-developed countries, and their sources, are given in Table 24. While the total receipts of the less-developed countries increased by about 30 percent over the period, and the receipts from industrial countries increased by about 23 percent, the flow from the industrial countries fell off in absolute terms from 1961 to 1963. Large as the magnitude of flow was in the early 1960's, it was substantially below the levels sought by the UN General Assembly resolution 1710 (XIV), as explained in the Secretary-General's report:[8]

> In so far as the resolution (of the UN General Assembly 1710 (XIV), calling for a maximum rate of growth of aggregate national income of 5 percent at the end of the 1960's) does provide a quantitative objective, it is to achieve a minimum annual rate of growth of aggregate national income of 5 per cent in all--or at the very least, the great majority--of the under-developed countries by 1970. It may perhaps be assumed that to achieve this minimum position at the end of the decade, the average rate of increase of the aggregate incomes of all under-developed countries during the remainder of the decade should not be less than 5 per cent and it would be desirable if towards the end of the decade it could be as high as 6 per cent or more. The magnitude of the global efforts required might be envisaged on the basis of these assumptions.
>
> The present best estimate is that the growth rate of national incomes of all under-developed countries, together, is about 3 1/2 per cent per year. The immediate task, therefore, will be to raise this growth rate during the coming few years by perhaps 1 1/2 per cent to at least 5 per cent and to increase this rate by a further 1 1/2 per cent to over 6 per cent per annum at the end of the decade.

TABLE 24

NET FLOW OF FUNDS TO LESS-DEVELOPED COUNTRIES, 1959-63

(Billions of Dollars)

	1959	1960	1961	1962	1963
Total from					
1. Industrial countries	7.3	8.2	9.6	8.9	9.0
A. Official bilateral, net	4.2	4.5	5.6	5.8	6.2
B. Private bilateral, net	2.6	2.8	3.0	2.2	2.5
C. Multilateral, net	.6	.9	1.0	.9	.4
2. Disbursements from multilateral agencies, net of capital repayments and subscriptions (A+B+C)	.3	.3	.3	.4	.7
3. Total receipts of less-developed countries (1A+B+2)	7.0	7.6	8.9	8.5	9.3

Source: Organisation for Economic Cooperation and Development, *The Flow of Financial Resources to Less-Developed Countries*, 1956-1963 (Paris: OECD, 1964), p.26.

If the increase to a 5 percent rate of growth seems large, it should be noted that the accomplishment would permit a doubling of the present standard of living--assuming a continuation of the present rate of population increase--within a period of twenty-five to thirty years.[9] In Asian, African, and Latin American countries the per capita income gain would be limited because of annual population gains of 3 to 3 1/2 percent.[10]

Viewed in the context of the world problem of economic development, efforts to restrict capital movements must be weighed carefully, since prevailing levels of capital receipts by less-developed countries are below the UN target level.[11] Much of the September, 1966, meeting of the World Bank (IBRD) was given over to the need for increased flows of development funds;[12] the fulfillment of this objective depended on loosening the strictures of balance of payments discipline. George Woods, President of the IBRD and the International Development Association (IDA), proposed an increase in the industrial nation quotas to IDA, bringing them to $1 billion from the present $250 million. The prospects of the proposal's being favorably considered in the near future are slight. The Managing Director of the IMF expressed regret that the industrial nations had become preoccupied with their own problems of economic growth, fighting inflation, and protecting balance of payments positions.[13]

STRUCTURAL CHANGE

The leg of U.S. balance of payments policy that sought change in the international monetary system was a response, not only to onerous pressures exerted on deficit countries by the international payments mechanism, but also a response to the strictures it placed on U.S. aid programs.[14] Implicit in the movement for changes in the Bretton Woods system was the argument that the adjustment process worked slowly (and, possibly, perversely) and required excessive internal changes in prices and incomes. The argument does not stand axiomatically, but the experience of the United States with its deficit-in-the-midst-of-price-stability-and-income-stability, and the experience of Britain with austerity programs, illustrate the twin stems of the argument for change.

U.S. sponsorship of changes in the Bretton Woods system to provide a systematic increase in world monetary reserves (liquidity), after many years of reluctance to consider changes in the system, has created a major source of world controversy. A brief outline of the proposals for change, and their important characteristics, will clarify the various positions taken by parties in the U.S. and abroad.

Proposals for Change in the Bretton Woods System

Nearly all of the proposals for changing the Bretton Woods gold-exchange standard system under which exchange rates are fixed, but subject to infrequent adjustment, have pointed to the haphazard process through which world liquidity (gold, convertible currencies, and IMF gold tranche) increases or decreases. In some recent years, nearly all of the increase in world liquidity has resulted from U.S. gold sales. Soviet gold sales, new gold production, foreign exchange increases, and increased reserve positions in the IMF are the other sources of world liquidity increase; and increased foreign exchange (chiefly bank deposits, a large part in the Eurodollar market) has contributed considerably to the total in recent years; of the $12.4 billion increase in world liquidity, 1958 to 1965, $5.7 billion was increases in foreign exchange, $3.9 billion increases in gold, and $2.8 billion increases in IMF reserve positions.[15] Gold production over these years totaled approximately $10 billion (at $35 per fine ounce), which indicates the relatively small proportion of new gold production that enters reserve holdings. Most new gold production goes into private use. World liquidity has been dependent in large part, therefore, on gold, dollars, and pounds supplied by balance of payments deficits of the U.S. and U.K., these being the chief key currency countries. Since key currency countries cannot run external deficit positions over long periods without destroying their key currency status an inherent instability exists in the prevailing system.[1] Only by running a surplus can the U.S. replenish its gold reserve; but a U.S. surplus will reduce world liquidity. This is the dilemma that creates the need for change in the world monetary system.

The proposals for change in the world monetary system occupy positions on a spectrum that extends from simple cooperative arrangements among central banks under the IMF, to basic modification of the IMF, and supplanting of the IMF altogether. Every proposal for change depends fundamentally on willingness of the major countries to consider changes from the viewpoint of international need rather than as a means of enhancing a world position. In the absence of supranational attitudes toward reform, little accomplishment can take place.

Cooperative Arrangements Within the IMF

The member countries of the IMF subscribe quotas composed normally of 25 percent gold and 75 percent their own currency. Up to the 25 percent "gold tranche," the Fund permits borrowing of foreign currencies virtually at will. If the member's currency is borrowed by other members, such that the original 75 percent is reduced, the member comes into additional borrowing rights, the "super gold tranche," equal to the difference between the currency proportion of his subscription and 75 percent. Drawing rights in "credit tranches" are normally equal to a country's quota, and the availability of these rights is governed by stricter rules. Credit tranche drawings are repaid when the drawer's position permits, but at most within three to five years. In June, 1966, stand-by arrangements to draw currencies from the Fund exceeded $6 billion, of which $4.4 remained to be drawn.

The drawing arrangements of the Fund--from which members had drawn $12.3 billion through June 30, 1966, $4.8 billion of which were outstanding--were supplemented in 1962 by the General Agreements to Borrow. By these agreements, the Group of Ten countries undertook to lend the Fund up to $6 billion of their currencies to augment drawing facilities. In addition, quota increases of 50 percent in 1959 and 25 percent in 1966 increased IMF quotas to $20.2 billion as of June 30, 1966; currency holdings totaled $17 billion and gold holdings (cumulative) $2.6 billion.[17] By increasing quotas, therefore, the

IMF has significantly supplemented world reserves. In 1958, when external convertibility was accomplished, IMF quotas were 9.7 percent of world export trade; in 1966 (first quarter), the percentage was 11.8.[18]

The IMF has considered means whereby reserves might be effectively increased through changes in its own policies. By ruling of the Executive Board, for example, drawing policies might be amended to permit virtually automatic borrowing to some limit beyond the present 100 percent of quota. This amendment might apply generally or to countries meeting certain criteria. The IMF would, in order to prevent contraction of conditional drawing facilities under this arrangement, have to seek an increase in quotas.

Mention should be made, in the context of cooperative arrangements, of the arrangements among central bank the Bank for International Settlements, and the OECD, that have developed since 1961. These arrangements have, on several occasions, prevented serious runs on currencies. The Basel Arrangements of 1961 and 1963, and the "swap" and other arrangements among the Group of Ten countries, given sufficient demonstration of need, afford the most flexible means for extending supplemental credits of a reserve-expanding type.

Modifications of the IMF Machinery

Other means for extending world reserves through IMF, which would require formal change in the Articles of Agreement, have been suggested. One procedure would empower the IMF to obtain special assets and assume additional liabilities, i.e., the Fund would borrow in international markets and create transferable assets with characteristics that made them as good as gold. This recommendation would extend a procedure similar to the General Agreements to Borrow or the holding by the IMF of U.S. Treasury Bills and Notes instead of gold. The amount of investment and asset creation could be arranged to grow at a stated percentage each year.

A close kin to this arrangement, but more daring, is the proposal to replace a portion of present reserve assets of a group of countries (probably the Group of Ten) with a new reserve asset, the Composite Reserve

Asset (CRU), which would be a form of "paper gold." The details of this proposal are varied. In the form urged by E.M. Bernstein,[19]

> ...the Reserve Unit, equal in value to $1 in gold, should be comprised of 80 cents in the currencies of the participating countries in agreed proportions. The remaining 20 cents of the Reserve Unit would be in the form of a claim on the Fund. The Reserve Units would be created by having the participating countries deposit their own currencies, in the agreed proportions, with the Fund as Trustee. Each country would be given a deposit credit in Reserve Units on the books of the Trustee equal to the amount of its own currency used as backing for the Reserve Unit. The Fund itself, not as a Trustee, would receive 20 percent of the Reserve Units created, contributing as backing its obligation in equal amount, to be met in gold or in the currencies of the participating countries whenever there is occasion to convert Reserve Units into their constituent currencies.
>
> Each country would undertake to hold Reserve Units in an agreed ratio to its gold reserves--say, $1 in Reserve Units to $2 in gold. Participating countries that hold reserves in dollars or other currencies would not hold Reserve Units jointly with such foreign exchange reserves. When a participating country with a balance-of-payments surplus presents the currency of another participating country for conversion, it would receive two-thirds of the amount in gold and one-third in Reserve Units. In order to avoid a too rapid expansion of reserves, the amount of Reserve Units created each year should be moderate, say, about $1 billion a year, until the agreed proportion to gold is reached. In this interim period countries would not have to hold the agreed ratio of Reserve Units to gold, but conversion of the currencies of the participating countries would be in the ratio of $2 in gold

> and $1 in Reserve Units.
>
> Under this proposal, the Fund would be allotted 20 percent of the Reserve Units created for the composite gold standard. As the Fund does not need Reserve Units for its own operations, it would sell its Reserve Units to the participating countries, getting in return their currencies. This will enable the Fund to build up its holdings of the currencies most widely used in its operations and thus to strengthen its liquidity to a significant extent. With the additional currencies it acquires from the creation and sale of Reserve Units, the Fund could be much more helpful in providing resources for its members to enable them to meet their reserve problems.
>
> The Reserve Units would be the instrument through which a participating surplus country would extend credit to a participating deficit country. In this respect, the credits granted under the composite gold standard would be similar to the credits these countries now make available to each other under the reciprocal currency arrangements.

Complex problems of participation by "members" in the increase or decrease of CRU assets, and the automaticity or conditionality of their availability, surround the proposal.[20] The establishment of a reserve center outside the IMF and restricted to major industrial nations has been criticized.[21] It is not clear what effect the CRU innovation would have on the adjustment process; so closely is the unit tied to gold, that much of the inflexibility associated with the gold standard seems to inhere in the "composite gold standard." The issue of oversufficiency of reserves--the "discipline problem"--will be considered at the close of this section.

Comprehensive Change in the IMF

In contrast to the proposals outlined above, the proposals for comprehensive (sometimes referred to as "drastic," or "radical") change would substitute for the Bretton Woods system a variant which, in some forms of the proposal, resembles Keynes' 1943 plan for a Clearing Union. The most familiar of these proposals is that of Professor Triffin.[22] In Triffin's proposal, the IMF would take on the character of an international central bank through which surpluses and deficits arising in international monetary relations would be cleared. Monetary reserves would be centralized in a mutual currency account within the IMF, and the Fund-bank would have powers to make loans and investments. The same problems--participation by "members" in the increase or decrease of reserves and the automaticity or conditionality of their availability--that surround other proposals for change in the international monetary system surround Triffin's ingenious proposal as well. Because the transformation of the IMF into a central banks' banking institution is a more fundamental change than the previously outlined proposals, and because it necessarily involves the surrender of national sovereignty over reserve assets, it has been the most controversial option with the least chance of adoption.

Appraising the Plans for Reform

Two major omissions detract from the attractiveness of the proposals outlined above: First, none of the proposals explicitly recognizes the reserve needs of the less-developed countries, and, second, none meets the problem of "discipline," the bringing to bear of incentive, in amounts neither too lax nor too strict, to remedy external imbalances.

Proposals of the Bernstein and Triffin types have only the probability of better operation of the international monetary system to offer less-developed countries. Other proposals, not discussed above, have been designed to expand the amount of credit available to these countries. A proposal by Sir Maxwell Stamp[23] attempted to expand liquidity and assure its distribution to less-developed countries; nonconvertible certificates denominated in gold would be issued by the IMF to international agencies established to coordinate aid. The certificates would be distributed by the agencies to less-developed countries and, when used by the recipients to settle external imbalances, would come into the possession of central banks and be accepted as "good-as-gold" reserves. Unfortunately, the proposal must counter the familiar objections with respect to amount of increase or decrease in "reserves," and the automaticity or conditionality of the certificate distribution. The plan, as originally proposed, had a definite inflationary bias.

Proposals for Change in the Adjustment Process

The proposals outlined thus far have sought to provide additional reserves through varying degrees of modification in prevailing practices within the IMF, or through basic change in the character of the IMF itself. Few of the authors of proposals for monetary reform explicitly concern themselves with the adjustment process as such. Nearly all of the proposals preserve a link between augmented reserve assets, or new assets, and gold, and the implication is that fixed parities in relation to gold would continue. A considerable sentiment exists for an approach to monetary reform which begins with the adjustment process, in a largely unmodified IMF, and leads into changes in the adjustment process. The argument proceeds along the lines employed to make the case for flexible exchange rates--fixed parities in a world ridden by commitments to full employment, price stability, and wages inflexible downward confound the adjustment process--but stops at a point between fixed and flexible rates. It is argued that merely a wider band of permissible variation in the gold-buying price and foreign exchange rates could restore a substantial degree of freedom of action to domestic monetary policy with a consequent unlocking of the adjustment forces.

Estimates of the degree of variation that should be sought in the gold price and exchange rates vary. Mundell has proposed a band of 7.5 percent,[24] while Halm, reviewing the wider band proposals, indicates that a 4 percent range would probably prove sufficient to counteract undesirable capital movements, but insufficient to influence trade transactions. The amount of band required is "a sufficient amount to accomplish the purpose," i.e., to frustrate undesirable movements of short-term capital by increasing the spot-forward spread and making cover expensive. Fortunately, the proposal lends itself to a process of gradual experimentation to arrive at appropriate band amounts.

This proposal is only one of many that see merit in a downward flexibility in the U.S. gold-buying price. Speculators on the world gold markets are, at present, the beneficiaries of a floor under the price of gold, which supports their presumption that the price will move upward, if it moves at all. Speculative hoarding is, therefore, promoted. By permitting some degree of downward adjustment of the U.S. gold-buying price, the one-way expectations of speculators might be changed, with the consequence that dishoarding would occur. This proposal would, of course, be of primary benefit to the United States in its key currency dilemma of recent years.

The pole opposite from proposals to weaken the role of gold-standard discipline in the international monetary system is the pole to strengthen it. By virtue of the possession of a large gold hoard, and a restless pursuit of grandeur, the French favor a gold-enhancing reform of the international monetary system. A variation on the CRU proposal appeals to General de Gaulle and his unofficial advisor, Jacques Rueff, and is, in fact, the only "reform" proposal that enjoys French support. Ten or twelve leading countries would in this proposal arrange for the issue (by the Bank for International Settlements) of CRU's linked to present gold holdings. The overhang of U.S. short-term liabilities, presently held by foreign official agencies, would be liquidated following a 100 percent increase in the gold price. A not unimportant immediate consequence of this proposal would be to give France a gold reserve equal to the United States. Future international imbalances would be settled by CRU's denominated in each country's currency and valued in ratio to each country's reserve share. The proposal has a deflationary bias, circumvents the IMF--the established international monetary body, creates a large-country club intended to run the international monetary system in its own interest, and appears to have been designed to accomplish General de Gaulle's goal of French grandeur in one step at the expense of the United States.

By mid-1965, the Group of Ten and the IMF had, independently, studied the need for monetary reform. The Group of Ten report,[25] known as the Ossala report, carefully summarized the arguments for, and against, the chief proposals for change in the international monetary system. Admitting to many divergences of view on the implications of the various plans, the Ossala report made no recommendations but listed four fundamental issues that created divergences of view:[26]

> (1) the question of the link between gold and the new reserve asset, the closeness of that link, and its effects on the existing system;
> (2) the width of membership for purposes of management and distribution of the assets;
> (3) the role of the IMF as regards deliberate reserve creation; and,
> (4) the rules for decision-making concerning the creation of reserve assets.

The divergences of view were great, indeed, and the prognosis for early modification of the international monetary system is pessimistic. In August, 1966, climaxing three years of discussion, the Group of Ten reported agreement on the need for reform, but no agreement on the type of reform.[27] A specific recommendation is sought for mid-1967. Meanwhile, the Kennedy Round tariff talks are stymied until mid-1967, an OECD report on European capital markets goes into its fourth year, and European monetary officials are renewing demands for an end to the U.S. deficit.[28]

The IMF annual report gave cautious indication that the proposals for reform had been narrowed to two polar opposites: deliberate creation of a new reserve asset, and/or extension of quasi-automatic drawing rights on the Fund.[29] It was reported, however, that the annual meeting of the Fund heard bitter dissent by France's Finance Minister, Michel Debre, from the proposal to continue the dollar as a reserve currency and supplement it with a new reserve asset, and only cautious endorsement of the proposal by Karl Blessing, Governor of the German Bundesbank.[30]

Not unexpectedly, there has arisen in the United States a resentment at the viewpoint, universally held among Continental European central bankers, which castigates U.S. international economic policies with the charge that the U.S. is avoiding the discipline function of the international payments system. This viewpoint holds U.S. deficits to be an aggravating factor in the control of inflationary pressures in the internal economies of Continental European countries. The emergence of the confidence problem that has arisen with respect to the dollar is traceable directly to European official agencies since they, rather than private holders of dollars, have chosen gold rather than dollars as the preferred international liquid asset.

The nub of the American protest can be put simply: Continental Europe has chosen to ignore the extenuating circumstances that caused the United States to develop a large overhang of liquid liabilities in the hands of foreign official monetary institutions. Forgotten, too, are the U.S. policies that were deliberately framed to relieve the burden of the dollar shortage in Europe. European monetary officials have now chosen to make a fetish of pristine gold-reserve currency ratios in their monetary reserves and, in so doing, have created doubts about the viability of the dollar and pressed the United States to adopt policies inimical to world trade, defense of the free world, and international monetary stability. Professor James Tobin has put the case against the U.S. detractors with characteristic directness:[31]

> Several courses were open to European countries whose central banks had to purchase dollars in their exchange markets in recent years. (a) They could have built up their dollar holdings quietly and gladly, as they did before 1959. (b) By exercising their right to buy gold at the United States Treasury, they could have forced devaluation of the dollar or suspension of gold payments. (c) They could have taken various measures to correct and reverse chronic European payments surpluses. (d) By occasional withdrawals of gold and by constant complaints they could have brought tremendous pressure for

> "discipline" upon the United States without forcing a change in the dollar parity.
>
> European central banks and governments chose the fourth course, with token admixtures of the third. They have made world opinion, and American opinion, believe there is no other choice. Almost everyone agrees that the pressure of the balance of payments deficit upon the United States is inescapable arithmetic rather than the deliberate policy of foreign governments. Yet for almost ten years previously, United States deficits were no problem. Clearly it is a change in human attitude and public policy, not inexorable circumstance, which has compelled us to take "corrective" actions.
>
> It is true that the concern of financial officials about "the dollar" was only an echo--and a subdued echo at that--of the fears, hopes, anxieties, and speculations that arose in private financial circles in the late 1950's. But financial officials do not have to follow the private exchange markets; they can lead instead. By an equivocal attitude toward private suspicions of the dollar, European officials kept pressure on the United States. Never did they firmly say that they would not force devaluation or suspension of gold payments. Instead, they succeeded in making the maintenance of gold-dollar convertibility at $35 per ounce a unilateral commitment of the United States, under three successive Administrations. Once a banker has solumnly assured the world and his depositors that he will never fail, he is at the mercy of those depositors capable of making him fail.
>
> Memories are short, and gratitude is not a consideration respected in international relations, especially when money is involved. But the United States had and has considerable moral claim on European governments and central banks.

Tobin, in the same vein, taunts U.S. officials for

accepting the European definition of the American predicament:[32]

> The United States has not pushed its moral case before world public opinion. This is because many Americans believe, or prefer to believe, that balance of payments deficits, like venereal diseases, betray and punish the sins of those whom they afflict. Others regard them as simply matters of arithmetic and circumstance. Still others are afraid that making a moral argument will indicate to our all-powerful European creditors insufficient resolution to overcome the difficulties. On their side, the Europeans have neatly segregated the contexts. Their financial officials wash their hands of tariff and trade policies, agricultural protection, defense and aid appropriations, and their governments' budgets. Any European failings on these counts are facts of life to which the United States must adjust, rather than reasons for more patience or more credit.

The growing reaction to European official pressure that has narrowed the range of effective U.S. policy choices is fed partly by resentment that U.S. international economic power has been abridged by the deficit, and partly by the irrationality of risking restriction of world trade growth merely to measure up to an arbitrary balance of payments criterion. Twenty years of gradual accomplishment in freeing international trade from encumbering controls--a task by no means complete--would be reversed to the detriment of all countries if the European prescription were to be followed. The dissent was slow to appear, but it is now an influential force in Washington policy-making. Three economists, each influential in U.S. policy-formulation, jointly published the dissenting view early in 1966.[33] After countering the European version of the meaning in the U.S. external imbalance, the trio called for a unilateral policy by the United States to restore a reserve-currency system, if necessary, using such tactics as widening the margin around the parity at which gold is bought and sold, reducing the gold price, and otherwise depriving gold of its present unlimited convertibility into dollars.[34]

Professor Despres has independently circulated a proposal that extends the "go it alone" approach to solving the world monetary problem.[35] In brief, Despres would limit the amount of gold the U.S. stands ready to buy at $35 an ounce to one-third of the present official holdings, with an offsetting introduction of credit to complement gold as a source of dollars, in the ratio of two of credit to one of gold.[36] Britain and the less-developed countries would be exempted. This proposal to partly demonetize gold would, according to Despres, reduce the price of gold because the price is presently determined by monetary gold use. Despres would solve the problem of the official overhang of dollars in official monetary reserves by inviting "the remaining reluctant official holders to convert into gold before we adopt the new gold plus credit formula."[37] This proposal is framed for the purpose of establishing a dollar-pound standard, to be accomplished by shifting asset preferences away from gold. The fact that the proposal is being studied in official circles is an indication that the range of options available to U.S. external policy is less limited than heretofore.

TRADE-OFFS AGAIN

The position of the United States, as the administration ponders a new course in international economic policy is one of interlocking dilemmas. Without the foreign exchange costs of the Vietnam War, the U.S. external position might have moved into the vicinity of zero net balance on official transactions in 1966. The outlook at present is for a net balance little different from the $1.3 billion deficit of 1965. Under the circumstances, the temptation will be to tighten capital outflow restrictions, possibly through capital controls, in order to create the "proper atmosphere" in which to press for monetary reform. There is an increasing danger that U.S. moves will restrict the growth of world trade and that constructive accomplishments twenty years in the making will be destroyed. Less-developed countries, which are pawns in the internecine struggle among industrial countries for external equilibrium, will face the choice of curtailing their expectations or giving vent to their frustrations. None of these outcomes is sought by the United States nor in its interest; and none of them is, in the present state of the dialogue on international monetary relations, available by exercise of United States power. A year or more hence, with the stability of the international monetary system continuously at stake in the interim, the time may be more propitious for a reordering of the system.

As the annual meetings of the International Monetary Fund and the World Bank convened in September, 1966, the Joint Economic Committee's Subcommittee on International Exchange and Payments, whose commissioned studies and deliberations are an important part of the documentation of the international monetary problem, sounded a warning and posed a challenge to the assembling delegates:[38]

> The world is in trouble--deep trouble--in at least five different areas of economic negotiation and policy: trade; aid to less-developed countries; maintaining a balance in international payments; international monetary reform; and maintenance of stable price levels in economies marked by full employment and rapid economic growth.
>
> . . .
>
> If the world's malaise were only economic, matters would be bad enough. But it is also political. The disintegration that has set in in recent years has gone across the full scope of diplomatic and military issues, as well as economic. Policies of the various countries have become increasingly preoccupied with shortrun nationalistic advantage rather than long-term international cooperation.

Notes to Chapter 6

1. Gunnar Myrdal, An International Economy (New York: Harper and Brothers, 1956), p.79.

2. In 1959 the IMF ruled that the spread between minimum and maximum spot rates might be as much as 4 percent whenever such a spread resulted from the

maintenance of margins of no more than 1 percent from parity for a convertible currency.

3. In 1961, the German mark and the Dutch guilder were revalued, and, in 1962, the Canadian dollar was devalued.

4. The literature on flexible exchange rates is large. Classic statements are James E. Meade, "The Case for Flexible Exchange Rates," The Three Banks Review (September, 1955), pp. 3-27, and Milton Friedman, "The Case for Flexible Exchange Rates," Essays in Positive Economics (Chicago: University of Chicago Press, 1953), pp. 157-203.

5. Belgium, Canada, France, West Germany, Italy, Japan, Netherlands, Sweden, United Kingdom, and the United States.

6. United Nations, The United Nations Development Decade, Proposals for Action (New York: United Nations, 1962), p. 5.

7. Organisation for Economic Cooperation and Development, op. cit., p. 85.

8. United Nations, op. cit., p. 8.

9. Ibid.

10. Ibid.

11. Cf. International Monetary Fund, 1966 Annual Report (Washington: International Monetary Fund, 1966), p. 5: "The flow of long-term financial resources to the less-developed countries has tended to stagnate in recent years."

12. Ibid.

13. The Journal of Commerce, September 27, 1966.

14. Tying of aid reduces the real value of aid receipts because it restricts purchases to one market instead of allowing the less-developed country to

shop around.

15. International Monetary Fund, International Financial Statistics (Washington: International Monetary Fund, August, 1966), p. 15.

16. Professor Leland B. Yeager comments on the threat posed by non-gold reserve build-up, as follows:

> Financial practice has now evolved beyond a mere pyramiding of deposit money in U.S. banks onto Federal Reserve funds, which are in turn pyramided onto gold. We now have the pyramiding of dollar deposits in European banks onto a fractional reserve of ordinary deposits in American banks, which are pyramided onto a fractional reserve of deposits in the Federal Reserve banks, which in turn are pyramided onto a fractional reserve of gold. And this is not all. Insofar as some foreign authorities peg their currencies to fractional reserves of foreign exchange consisting partly of Eurodollars rather than entirely of ordinary dollars, foreign currencies are pyramided onto a fractional reserve of Eurodollars, which are pyramided fractionally onto ordinary dollar deposits, which are pyramided fractionally onto Federal Reserve deposits, which are in turn pyramided fractionally onto gold.

Leland B. Yeager, International Monetary Relations (New York and Evanston: Harper and Row, 1966), p. 470.

17. International Monetary Fund, International Financial Statistics (Washington: International Monetary Fund, August, 1966), p. 15.

18. Ibid., pp. 8, 16-17.

19. E.M. Bernstein, "The Underdeveloped Countries and Monetary Reserves," in Joint Economic Committee, Guidelines for International Monetary Reform, Part 2, Supplement (Washington: Joint Economic Committee, 1965),

pp. 278-79.

20. Group of Ten, *Report of the Study Group on the Creation of Reserve Assets* (Washington: The Government Printing Office, 1965).

21. *Ibid.*, pp. 60-66.

22. Robert Triffin, *Gold and the Dollar Crisis* (New Haven: Yale University Press, 1960).

23. Herbert B. Grubel, ed., *World Monetary Reform* (Stanford: Stanford University Press, 1963), pp. 80-89.

24. Robert A. Mundell, "The International Monetary System: Conflict and Reform," in Joint Economic Committee, *op. cit.*, p. 465, and George N. Halm, "The 'Band Proposal': The Limits of Permissible Exchange Rate Fluctuation," in *ibid.*, p. 532.

25. Group of Ten, *op. cit.*, pp. 51-78.

26. *Ibid.*, p. 95.

27. *New York Times*, August 28, 1966.

28. *Journal of Commerce*, April 8, 1966.

29. International Monetary Fund, *1966 Annual Report* (Washington: International Monetary Fund, 1966), p. 9.

30. *New York Times*, September 28, 1966.

31. James Tobin, "Europe and the Dollar," *The Review of Economics and Statistics*, XLVI (May, 1964), pp. 123-24.

32. *Ibid.*, pp. 124-25.

33. Emile Despres, Charles P. Kindleberger, and Walter S. Salant, "*The Dollar and World Liquidity, A Minority View*," reprinted with additional material from *The Economist* (London), February 5, 1966 (Washington: The Brookings Institution, April, 1966).

34. *Ibid.*, p. 11.

35. Emile Despres, "Proposal Re Change in U.S. Gold Policy," in Joint Economic Committee, *op. cit.*, pp. 548-61.

36. *Ibid.*, pp. 552-53.

37. *Ibid.*

38. Joint Economic Committee, *Twenty Years After: An Appeal for the Renewal of International Economic Co-operation on a Grand Scale* (Washington: Joint Economic Committee, 1966), pp. 1, 3.

BIBLIOGRAPHY

Books

Abs, Hermann J. _The European Security and New Issues Market with a View to International Financing_ (Frankfurt: Deutsche Bank, A.G., 1964).

Adler, John H.; Schlesinger, Eugene R.; and Van Westerborg, Evelyn. _The Pattern of United States Import Trade Since 1923_ (New York: Federal Reserve Bank of New York, 1948).

Balogh, Thomas. "The United States and International Economic Equilibrium," _Foreign Economic Policy for the United States_, Seymour E. Harris (ed.) (Cambridge: Harvard University Press, 1948).

Basch, Antonin. _Capital Markets of the European Economic Community_ (Ann Arbor: University of Michigan, 1965).

Belof, Max. _The United States and the Unity of Europe_ (Washington: The Brookings Institution, 1963).

Bloomfield, Arthur I. _Capital Imports and the American Balance of Payments 1934-39_ (Chicago: University of Chicago Press, 1950).

_______. _Monetary Policy Under the International Gold Standard 1880-1914_ (New York: Federal Reserve Bank of New York, 1959).

Crump, Norman. _The ABC of the Foreign Exchanges_ (London: Macmillan, 1963).

Einzig, Paul A. _A Dynamic Theory of Forward Exchange_ (London: Macmillan, 1961).

_______. _The Euro-Dollar System: Practice and Theory of International Interest Rates_ (London: Macmillan, 1964).

Ellis, Howard S., and Metzler, Lloyd A. (eds.). Readings in the Theory of International Trade (Philadelphia: The Blakiston Company, 1950).

Friedman, Milton, and Schwartz, Anna Jacobson. A Monetary History of the United States 1867-1960 (Princeton: Princeton University Press, 1963).

Gardner, Richard N. Sterling-Dollar Diplomacy (Oxford: The Clarendon Press, 1956).

Gayer, Arthur D. Monetary Policy and Economic Stabilization (2nd ed.; New York: Macmillan, 1937).

Haberler, Gottfried, and Stern, Robert (eds.). Equilibrium and Growth in the World Economy, Economic Essays by Ragnar Nurkse (Cambridge: Harvard University Press, 1961).

Harris, Seymour E. (ed.). The Dollar in Crisis (New York: Harcourt Brace, 1961).

Harrod, R. F. Life of John Maynard Keynes (New York: Harcourt Brace, 1951).

Hull, Cordell. Memoirs of Cordell Hull (2 vols.; New York: Macmillan, 1948).

Keynes, John Maynard. Indian Currency and Finance (London: Macmillan, 1913).

_______. Monetary Reform (New York: Harcourt Brace, 1924).

Kindleberger, Charles P. International Economics (Homewood, Illinois: Irwin Co., 1958).

Krause, Lawrence B., and Dam, Kenneth W. Federal Tax Treatment of Foreign Income (Washington: The Brookings Institution, 1964).

Lary, Hal B. Problems of the United States as World Trader and Banker (New York: National Bureau of Economic Research, Inc., 1963).

Machlup, Fritz. International Payments, Debts and Gold (New York: Charles Scribner's Sons, 1964).

Meade, James E. The Balance of Payments (Oxford: Oxford University Press, 1951).

Morgenstern, Oskar. International Financial Transactions and Business Cycles (Princeton: Princeton University Press, 1959).

Myrdal, Gunnar. An International Economy Problems and Prospects (New York: Harper and Brothers, 1956).

Nurkse, Ragnar. International Currency Experience (Princeton: League of Nations, 1944).

Penrose, E. F. Economic Planning for the Peace (Princeton: Princeton University Press, 1953).

Portmann, Heinz. Ansatze zu einem europäischem Kapitalmarkt (Zurich: Schweizerische Bankgesellschaft, 1965).

Robertson, Dennis H. Britain in the World Economy (London: Allen and Unwin, 1954).

Roosa, Robert V. Monetary Reform for the World Economy (New York and Evanston: Harper and Row, 1965).

Salant, Walter S., et. al. The United States Balance of Payments in 1968 (Washington: The Brookings Institution, 1963).

Scammell, W. M. International Monetary Policy (2nd ed.; London: Macmillan, 1961).

Shannon, Ian. International Liquidity (Chicago: Henry Regnery Co., 1964).

Tinbergen, Jan. Lessons from the Past (Amsterdam: Elsevier Publishing Co., 1963).

_______. Shaping the World Economy (New York: Twentieth Century Fund, 1962).

Triffin, Robert. Europe and the Money Muddle (New Haven: Yale University Press, 1957).

_______. Gold and the Dollar Crisis (New Haven: Yale University Press, 1960).

Twentieth Century Fund. The New Europe and Its Economic Future (New York: Macmillan, 1964).

Wasserman, Max J.; Hultman, Charles W.; and Zsoldas, Laslo. International Finance (New York: Simmons-Boardman Publishing Corp., 1963).

Williams, John H. Economic Stability in the Modern World (London: Athlone Press, 1952).

Articles

Allen, R. G. D. "Statistics of the Balance of Payments," Economic Journal, LXI (March, 1951), pp. 179-96.

Altman, Oscar L. "Euro-Dollars: Some Further Comments," International Monetary Fund, Staff Papers, XII (March, 1965), pp. 1-16.

_______. "Foreign Markets for Dollars, Sterling and Other Currencies," International Monetary Fund, Staff Papers, VIII (December, 1961), pp.313-52.

_______. "Recent Developments in Foreign Markets for Dollars and Other Currencies," International Monetary Fund, Staff Papers, X (March, 1963), pp. 48-96.

Angell, James W. "The Reorganization of the International Monetary System: An Alternative Proposal," Economic Journal, LXXI (December, 1961), pp. 691-708.

Behrman, Jack N. "Foreign Private Investment and the Government's Efforts to Reduce the Payments Deficit," Journal of Finance, XXI (May, 1966), pp. 283-96.

Bernstein, E. M. "The Adequacy of the United States Gold Reserves," American Economic Review, Papers and Proceedings, LI (May, 1961), pp. 439-46.

Board of Governors of the Federal Reserve System. "Treasury and Federal Reserve Foreign Exchange Operations," Monthly Review of the Federal Reserve Bank of New York, 45 (September, 1963), pp. 162-72.

_______. "Treasury and Federal Reserve Foreign Exchange Operations and the Gold Pool," Federal Reserve Bulletin (March, 1964), pp. 294-307.

Clement, M. O. "A Functional Approach to the Concept of International Reserves," Kyklos, XVI (1963), pp. 415-35.

Coombs, Charles A. "Treasury and Federal Reserve Foreign Exchange Operations," Monthly Review of the Federal Reserve Bank of New York, 42 (September, 1962), pp. 1138-53.

Delcourt, Jean-Paul. "Means by Which the State Can Influence Economic Development Under the Plan," French and Other National Plans (Paris: Comite Europeen et Social, 1963), pp. 23-27.

Despres, Emile, et. al. "The Dollar and World Liquidity, A Minority View," reprint from The Economist, February 5, 1966 (Washington: The Brookings Institution, April, 1966).

de Wilmars, Jacques Mertens. "Währungsperspectiven des Gemeinsamen Marktes," Weltwirtschaftliches Archiv, 90 (1963), pp. 350-76.

Egle, Walter P. "American Reaction to the Balance of Payments Deficit," Weltwirtschaftliches Archiv, 93 (1964), pp. 273-85.

_______. "The Four Approaches to Monetary Reform: A Critique," Zeitschrift für Nationalokonomie, XXII (1963), pp. 1-19.

Flanders, M. June. "The Balance-of-Payments Adjustment Mechanism: Some Problems in Model-Building,"

Kyklos, XVI (1963), pp. 395-414.

Fleming, Marcus. "The Fund and International Liquidity," International Monetary Fund, Staff Papers, XI (July, 1964), pp. 177-215.

Frankel, Marvin. "Home Versus Foreign Investment: A Case Against Capital Export," Kyklos, XVIII (1965), pp. 411-33.

Friedman, Irving S. "The International Monetary System, Part I: Mechanism and Operation," International Monetary Fund, Staff Papers, X (July, 1963), pp. 219-45.

Gardner, Walter R. "An Exchange Market Analysis of the U.S. Balance of Payments," International Monetary Fund, Staff Papers, VIII (May, 1961), pp. 195-221.

Gatz, Werner. "Reasons and Economic Consequences of the Revaluation of the Deutsche Mark," Weltwirtschaftliches Archiv, 90 (1963), pp. 379-431.

Gordon, Wendell. "The Criterion for an Adverse Balance of Payments," American Economic Review, LII (March, 1963), pp. 139-41.

Hackett, John. "Planning for Growth: The French Experiment," OECD Observer (June, 1963), pp. 9-14.

Harrod, Roy F. "Europe and the Money Muddle," Economic Journal, LXVIII (September, 1958), pp. 534-38.

Hogan, John D. "A New Tax Tool: The Interest Equalization Tax," Proceedings of the Fifty-Eighth National Tax Conference (Harrisburg: National Tax Association, 1966), pp. 563-72.

_______. "Western European Capital Markets and the Role of Life Insurance Companies," Journal of Risk and Insurance, 31 (June, 1964), pp. 157-68.

_______. "Western European Capital Markets and U.S. Capital Outflow Restriction," The Quarterly Review of Economics and Business, 4 (Summer, 1964), pp. 65-78.

Holbik, Karel. "West German Development Aid--The Means and Ends," The Quarterly Review of Economics and Business, 5 (Winter, 1965), pp. 5-19.

Horsefield, J. Keith. "International Liquidity," Finance and Development, I (December, 1964), pp. 170-77.

Høst-Madsen, Paul. "Asymmetries Between Balance of Payments Surpluses and Deficits," International Monetary Fund, Staff Papers, IX (July, 1962), pp. 182-201.

_______. "Gold Outflows from the United States, 1958-63," International Monetary Fund, Staff Papers, XI (July, 1964), pp. 248-61.

Hume, L. J. "The Gold Standard and Deflation: Issues and Attitudes in the Nineteen-Twenties," Economica (August, 1963), pp. 225-42.

Johnson, Harry G. "The Decade Ahead--In U.S. International Economic Relations," The Journal of Business of the University of Chicago, XXXVIII (July, 1965), pp. 245-51.

Kaldor, Nicholas. "The Problems of International Liquidity," Bulletin of the Oxford Institute of Economics and Statistics, 26 (1964), pp. 275-87.

Kenen, Peter B. "Nature, Capital and Trade," Journal of Political Economy, LXXIII (October, 1963), pp. 437-60.

Kindleberger, Charles P. "European Economic Integration and the Development of a Single Financial Center for Long-Term Capital," Weltwirtschaftliches Archiv, 90 (1963), pp. 189-208.

Lederer, Walther. "The Balance of Payments in 1963," Survey of Current Business, 44 (March, 1964), pp. 14-23.

_______. "Measuring the Balance of Payments," 1961 Proceedings of the Business and Economic Statistics Section (Washington: American Statistical Association, 1962), pp. 42-46.

Lubbert, Jens. "Internationale Kapitalbewegungen als Problem und Instrument der Zählungsbilanzpolitik," Weltwirtschaftliches Archiv, 91 (1963), pp. 61-83.

Meade, James E. "The Case for Variable Exchange Rates," Three Banks Review (September, 1955), pp. 3-27.

Meltzer, Allan H. "Improvement in the Balance of Payments: A Response to Monetary Policy or to Ad Hoc Fiscal Policies," The Journal of Business of the University of Chicago, XXXVIII (July, 1965), pp. 267-76.

Metzler, Lloyd A. "Exchange Rates and the International Monetary Fund," Lloyd A. Metzler, Robert Triffin, and Gottfried Haberler, International Monetary Policies (Washington: Board of Governors of the Federal Reserve System, 1947), pp. 1-44.

______. "The Transfer Problem Reconsidered," Journal of Political Economy, 50 (1942), pp. 397-414.

Modigliani, Franco, and Kenen, Peter B. "A Suggestion for Solving the International Liquidity Problem," Banca Nazionale de Lavoro Quarterly Review, 76 (March, 1966), pp. 3-17.

Mundell, Robert A. "The Appropriate Use of Monetary and Fiscal Policy for Internal and External Stability," International Monetary Fund, Staff Papers, IX (March, 1962), pp. 70-79.

______. "Problems of Monetary and Exchange Rate Management in Canada," National Banking Review, 2 (September, 1964), pp. 77-86.

Pederson, Jorgen. "The Problem of International Liquidity," Weltwirtschaftliches Archiv (1965), pp. 178-87.

Robinson, Joan. "The International Currency Proposals," Economic Journal, LIII (1943), pp. 161-75.

Romanis, Anne. "Balance of Payments Adjustment Among Developed Countries," International Monetary Fund, Staff Papers, XII (March, 1965), pp. 17-36.

Rueff, Jacques. "The West is Risking a Credit Collapse," Fortune, LXIV (July, 1961), pp. 126ff.

Salant, Walter S. A New Look at the U.S. Balance of Payments (Washington: The Brookings Institution, 1965).

Salin, Edgar. "Für eine europäische Währung," J.C.B. Mohr, and Paul Liebeck (eds.), Fundamentale Fragen kunftiger Währungspolitik (Tübingen: 1965), pp. 199-219.

Salin, P. "The Flexible Exchange Rate Controversy and the Problem of Simultaneous Internal and External Balance," Economica Internazionale (November, 1965), pp.371-412.

Shapiro, Eli, and Solomon, Ezra. "International Monetary Relations," The Southern Economic Journal (January, 1950), pp. 310-25.

Snider, Delbert A. "The Case for Capital Controls to Relieve the U.S. Balance of Payments," American Economic Review, LIV (June, 1964), pp. 346-58.

Staley, Charles E. "International Liquidity and American Policy," Kyklos, XVII (1964), pp. 470-78.

Stern, Robert M. "International Compensation for Fluctuations in Commodity Trade," The Quarterly Journal of Economics, LXXVII (May, 1943), pp. 258-73.

Streeten, Paul. "Common Fallacies About the Common Market," Weltwirtschaftliches Archiv, 90 (1963), pp. 276-89.

Triffin, Robert. "The Bizarre Proposals of Dr. Bernstein for International Monetary Reform," Kyklos, XVIII (1964), pp. 328-45.

_______. "National Central Banking and the International Economy," Lloyd A. Metzler, Robert Triffin, and Gottfried Haberler, International Monetary Policies (Washington: Board of Governors of the Federal Reserve System, 1947), pp. 46-81.

_______. "The Presentation of the U.S. Balance of Payments Statistics, General Comments," 1961 Proceedings of the Business and Economic Statistics Section (Washington: American Statistical Association, 1962), pp. 51-52.

Turot, Paul. "Le Marche des Capitaux a Court Terme en Europe et l'Euro-Dollar," Banque (Paris: April, 1961), pp. 215ff.

Vanek, Jaroslav. "Unilateral Trade Liberalization and Global World Income," The Quarterly Journal of Economics, LXXVIII (February, 1964), pp. 139-47.

White, William H. "Interest Rate Differences, Forward Exchange Mechanism, and Scope for Short-Term Capital Movements," International Monetary Fund, Staff Papers, X (November, 1963), pp. 485-503.

_______. "Regulation of Short-Term Interest Rates Through Monetary Action," International Monetary Fund, Staff Papers, X (July, 1963), pp. 299-320.

Williams, David. "The Development of Capital Markets in Europe," International Monetary Fund, Staff Papers, XII (March, 1965), pp. 37-62.

Reports, Monographs, and Government Publications

Bank for International Settlements. Annual Report (Basel: Bank for International Settlements, 1946-66).

Bell, Philip W. "Private Capital Movements and the U.S. Balance of Payments Position," Factors Affecting the United States Balance of Payments (Washington: Joint Economic Committee, 1962), pp. 395-481.

Bernstein, E. M. "A Supplementary Note on the Balance of Payments Statistics," The Balance of Payments Statistics (Washington: Joint Economic Committee, 1965), pp. 289-93.

_______. International Effects of U.S. Economic Policy (Washington: Joint Economic Committee, 1960).

Bowie, Robert R., and Geiger, Theodore. The European Economic Community and the United States (Washington: Joint Economic Committee, 1961).

Brookings Institution. Development of American Policy Toward the Unity of Europe (Washington: Brookings Institution, 1963).

Bundesminister fur Wirtschaft. Die Wirtschaftliche Lage in der Bundesrepublik Deutschland (Bonn: Bundesminister für Wirtschaft, 1960-65).

Commission on Foreign Economic Policy. Staff Papers Presented to the Commission on Foreign Economic Policy (Washington: Commission on Foreign Economic Policy, 1956).

Conseil National du Credít. Compte Rendu Trimistriel (Paris: Conseil National du Credít, 1960-65).

Cooper, Richard N. The Interest Equalization Tax: An Experiment in the Separation of Capital Markets (New Haven: Yale University Economic Growth Center, 1966).

Council of Economic Advisors. Economic Report of the President; Transmitted to the Congress January, 1966 (Washington: Council of Economic Advisors, 1966).

Department of Commerce. The Balance of Payments of the United States: 1949-1951. A Supplement to the Survey of Current Business (Washington: Department of Commerce, 1952).

_______. Foreign Business Investment in the United States. A Supplement to the Survey of Current Business (Washington: Department of Commerce, 1962).

_______. Foreign Investments in the United States. A Supplement to the Survey of Current Business (Washington: Department of Commerce, 1953).

_______. U.S. Business Investment in Foreign Countries. A Supplement to the Survey of Current Business (Washington: Department of Commerce, 1960).

Department of Labor. "Unit Labor Costs in Nine Countries," Monthly Labor Review (Washington: Department of Labor, September, 1965), pp. 1056-68.

Deutsche Bundesbank. Monthly Report (Bonn: Deutsche Bundesbank, 1960-66).

Economic Research Group of the Amsterdam-Rotterdam Bank N.V., Deutsche Bank AG, Midland Bank, and Societe Generale de Banque: Generale Bank Maatschappis. Capital Markets in Europe (London: Economic Research Group, 1966).

Eiteman, Wilford J., and Eiteman, David K. Leading World Stock Exchanges (Ann Arbor: University of Michigan, 1964).

Federal Minister of Economic Affairs. Report on Economic Trends in 1962 and Prospects for 1963 (Bonn: Ministry of Economic Affairs, 1963).

Federal Reserve Bank of New York. Annual Report for 1945-65 (New York: Federal Reserve Bank of New York, 1946-66).

_______. Federal Reserve Operations in the Money and Government Securities Markets (New York: Federal Reserve Bank of New York, 1956).

Haberler, Gottfried. "A Survey of International Trade Theory," Special Papers on International Economics, 1 (Princeton: Princeton University Press, September, 1955).

Halm, George N. "Special Problems of a Key Currency in Balance-of-Payments Deficit," Factors Affecting the United States Balance of Payments (Washington: Joint Economic Committee, 1962), pp. 543-61.

Herter, Christian A., and Clayton, William L. A New Look at Foreign Economic Policy In Light of the Cold War and the Extension of the Common Market in Europe (Washington: Joint Economic Committee, 1961).

Holmes, Alan R. The New York Foreign Exchange Market (New York: Federal Reserve Bank of New York, 1959).

House of Lords. Parliamentary Debates on an International Clearing Union (London: House of Lords, May 18, 1943).

International Bank for Reconstruction and Development. Second Annual Report of the Executive Directors (Washington: International Bank for Reconstruction and Development, 1947).

International Monetary Fund. Articles of Agreement (Washington: International Monetary Fund, 1965).

_______. Balance of Payments Manual (3rd ed.; Washington: International Monetary Fund, 1961).

_______. Balance of Payments Yearbook (Washington: International Monetary Fund, 1960-64).

_______. By-Laws, Rules and Regulations, 25th Issue (Washington: International Monetary Fund, June, 1954).

_______. International Reserves and Liquidity (Washington: International Monetary Fund, 1958).

_______. Summary Proceedings, Annual Meeting (Washington: International Monetary Fund, 1965).

_______. "The Management of International Liquidity," International Monetary Fund, Staff Papers, XI, 2 (Washington: International Monetary Fund, July, 1964).

_______. 1965 Annual Report (Washington: International Monetary Fund, 1965).

_______. 1966 Annual Report (Washington: International Monetary Fund, 1966).

Joint Economic Committee. The Balance of Payments Statistics. Hearings before the Subcommittee on Economic Statistics, Parts I and II (Washington: Joint Economic Committee, 1965).

_______. The Balance of Payments Statistics of the United States. Report of the Subcommittee on Economic Statistics (Washington: Joint Economic Committee, July, 1965).

_______. Economic Policies and Practices: A Description and Analysis of Certain European Capital Markets, Paper No. 3 (Washington: Joint Economic Committee, 1964).

_______. Factors Affecting the United States Balance of Payments. Compilation of Studies Prepared for the Subcommittee on International Exchange and Payments (Washington: Joint Economic Committee, 1962).

_______. Guidelines for Improving the International Monetary System, Parts I and II (Washington: Joint Economic Committee, 1965).

______. Guidelines for International Monetary Reform. Hearings before the Subcommittee on International Exchange and Payments, Part 2, Supplement (Washington: Joint Economic Committee, 1965).

______. International Effects of U.S. Economic Policy, Paper No. 16 (Washington: Joint Economic Committee, 1960).

______. International Payments Imbalances and Need for Strengthening International Financial Arrangements. Hearings before the Subcommittee on International Exchange and Payments, May 16, June 19, 20, and 21, 1961 (Washington: Joint Economic Committee, 1961).

______. International Payments Imbalances and Need for Strengthening International Financial Arrangements. Report of the Subcommittee on International Exchange and Payments (Washington: Joint Economic Committee, August, 1961).

______. Outlook for the United States Balance of Payments. Hearings before the Subcommittee on International Exchange and Payments, December 12, 13, and 14, 1962 (Washington: Joint Economic Committee, 1963).

______. The United States Balance of Payments. Part 3, The International Monetary System: Functioning and Possible Reform. Hearings before the Joint Economic Committee, November 12, 13, 14, and 15, 1963 (Washington: Joint Economic Committee, 1963).

______. The United States Balance of Payments: Statements by Economists, Bankers, and Others on the Brookings Institution Study, The United States Balance of Payments in 1968 (Washington: Joint Economic Committee, November, 1963).

Kenen, Peter B. "Reserve-Asset Preferences of Central Banks and Stability of the Gold Exchange Standard," Princeton Studies in International Finance, 10 (Princeton: Princeton University, 1963).

Klopstock, Fred H. "The International Status of the Dollar," Essays in International Finance, 28 (Princeton: Princeton University, 1957).

Kravis, Irwin B. The U.S. Trade Position and the Common Market (Washington: Joint Economic Committee, 1962).

Machlup, Fritz. "Plans for the Reform of the International Monetary System," Special Papers in International Economics, 3 (Princeton: Princeton University, August, 1963).

Mikesell, Raymond F., and Allen, Robert L. Economic Policies Toward Less-Developed Countries (Washington: Joint Economic Committee, 1961).

Ministré des Finances. Quelques Aspects du Probleme de l'Or, Cahiers de l'Institut de Science Economique Appliquee, Series R., No. 7 (Paris Ministré des Finances, 1962).

_______. Rapport par le Comité Charge d'Etudier le Financement des Investissements (Paris: Ministré des Finances, May, 1963).

_______. Statistiques et Etudes Finances, Supplement, Seizieme Rapport Annual de Conseil National du Credít (Paris: Ministré des Finances, August, 196[illegible]

Nurske, Ragnar. "Conditions of International Monetary Equilibrium," Essays in International Finance, 4 (Princeton: Princeton University, 1945).

Organisation for Economic Cooperation and Development. The Balance of Payments Adjustment Process (Paris: Organisation for Economic Cooperation and Development, 1966).

_______. Code for Liberalisation of Capital Movements (Paris: Organisation for Economic Cooperation and Development, June, 1965).

_______. Economic Surveys: Belgium-Luxembourg Economic Union (Paris: Organisation for

Economic Cooperation and Development, 1965).

_______. Economic Surveys: France (Paris: Organisation for Economic Cooperation and Development, 1965).

_______. Economic Surveys: Germany (Paris: Organisation for Economic Cooperation and Development, 1965).

_______. Economic Surveys: Italy (Paris: Organisation for Economic Cooperation and Development, 1965).

_______. Economic Surveys: United States (Paris: Organisation for Economic Cooperation and Development, 1965).

_______. The Flow of Financial Resources to Less-Developed Countries, 1956-1963 (Paris: Organisation for Economic Cooperation and Development, 1964).

_______. Ministerial Statement of the Group of Ten and Annex Prepared by Deputies (Paris: Organisation for Economic Cooperation and Development, 1964).

Organization for European Economic Cooperation. Statistics of National Produce and Expenditure (Paris: Organization for European Economic Cooperation, 1966).

Reischer, Otto R. Trade Adjustment in Theory and Practice (Washington: Joint Economic Committee, 1961).

Review Committee for Balance of Payments Statistics. The Balance of Payments Statistics of the United States (Washington: U.S. Government Printing Office, 1965).

Roosa, Robert V. "The Beginning of a New Policy," Emergence of an American Balance of Payments Policy (Washington: Joint Economic Committee, 1962), pp. 327-32.

Treasury Department. Treasury Bulletin (Washington: U.S. Treasury Department, August issues, 1960-66).

Triffin, Robert. "The Evolution of the International Payments System: Historical Reappraisal and Future Perspectives," Princeton Studies in International Finance, 12 (Princeton: Princeton University, 1964).

United Nations. Balance of Payments 1939-45 (Geneva: United Nations, 1948).

_______. The Growth of World Industry, 1938-61, International Analysis and Tables (New York: United Nations, 1965).

_______. Towards a New Trade Policy for Development (New York: United Nations, 1964).

_______. The United Nations Development Decade (New York: United Nations, 1962).

INDEX

ABOUT THE AUTHOR

John D. Hogan has been Staff Economist for the Northwestern Mutual Life Insurance Company, Milwaukee, Wisconsin, since 1960. Previously he taught economics on the staffs of Syracuse University, Russell Sage College, and Bates College. For the past four years he has taught monetary theory and policy as a lecturer in the Graduate School of Business, Marquette University, and in the Department of Economics, University of Wisconsin-Milwaukee. He received bachelor's, master's, and doctorate degrees in economics from the Maxwell School, Syracuse University.

Dr. Hogan's research in the field of balance of payments policy resulted in the publication of two articles in 1964,[1] among the first to appear on the relationship of the U.S. deficit to borrowing by Western European countries in the New York market. To further this research interest Dr. Hogan visited major European capital markets during the summer of 1965, holding conferences and conducting seminars in Frankfurt, Zurich, Rome, Geneva, Paris, Brussels, Rotterdam, and Amsterdam. This volume is largely the product of that effort.

[1] John D. Hogan, "Western European Capital Markets and U.S. Capital Outflow Restriction," _The Quarterly Review of Economics and Business_, IV (1964), and "Western European Capital Markets," _Journal of Risk and Insurance_, XXXI (1964).

Friendship Libr/Fairleigh Dickinson Univ
Madison, NJ 07940
3 3208 00320 4567